Handbook of
Township
Management
The Singapore Model

Highly Recommended Titles by World Scientific

Home, Truly: Building Dreams, Housing Hopes
by Housing & Development Board
ISBN: 978-981-123-063-9

50 Years of Urban Planning in Singapore
edited by Chye Kiang Heng
ISBN: 978-981-4656-45-0
ISBN: 978-981-4656-46-7 (pbk)

Singapore's Real Estate: 50 Years of Transformation
edited by Ngee Huat Seek, Tien Foo Sing and Shi Ming Yu
ISBN: 978-981-4689-25-0
ISBN: 978-981-4689-26-7 (pbk)

*Housing and Commuting: The Theory of Urban Residential Structure —
A Textbook in Urban Economics*
edited by John Yinger
ISBN: 978-981-3206-65-6
ISBN: 978-981-3206-66-3 (pbk)

Handbook of Township Management
The Singapore Model

Teo Ho Pin

National University of Singapore, Singapore
Singapore University of Social Sciences, Singapore &
Singapore University of Technology and Design, Singapore

World Scientific

NEW JERSEY · LONDON · SINGAPORE · BEIJING · SHANGHAI · HONG KONG · TAIPEI · CHENNAI · TOKYO

Published by

World Scientific Publishing Co. Pte. Ltd.

5 Toh Tuck Link, Singapore 596224

USA office: 27 Warren Street, Suite 401-402, Hackensack, NJ 07601

UK office: 57 Shelton Street, Covent Garden, London WC2H 9HE

National Library Board, Singapore Cataloguing in Publication Data
Name(s): Teo, Ho Pin.
Title: Handbook of township management : the Singapore model / Teo Ho Pin.
Description: Singapore : World Scientific Publishing Co. Pte. Ltd., [2023]
Identifier(s): ISBN 978-981-12-7407-7 (hardcover) | ISBN 978-981-12-7529-6 (paperback) |
  ISBN 978-981-12-7408-4 (ebook for institutions) |
  ISBN 978-981-12-7409-1 (ebook for individuals)
Subject(s): LCSH: City councils--Singapore. | Facility management--Singapore. |
  Cities and towns--Singapore.
Classification: DDC 307.76068--dc23

British Library Cataloguing-in-Publication Data
A catalogue record for this book is available from the British Library.

For any available supplementary material, please visit
https://www.worldscientific.com/worldscibooks/10.1142/13346#t=suppl

Desk Editor: Jiang Yulin

Typeset by Stallion Press
Email: enquiries@stallionpress.com

Contents

Acknowledgements   ix
Note from the Author   xi
Preface   xiii

Chapter 1 Introduction of Town Council in Singapore   **1**

1.1 Public Housing in Singapore   1
1.2 Concept of Town Council   1
1.3 Formation of Town Council   3
1.4 Purpose of Town Council   3
1.5 Key Stakeholders of Town Council   4
1.6 Desired Outcomes of Town Council
    Management   9
1.7 Key Business Functions of Town Council Management   12
1.8 Key Performance Indicators of Town Council Management   17
1.9 Proceedings of Town Council   20

Chapter 2 Town Council Governance   **27**

2.1 Introduction   27
2.2 Town Councils Act   27
2.3 Town Councils Financial Rules   42
2.4 Town Council By-laws   44
2.5 Town Council Code of Governance   48

Chapter 3 Town Council Setup, Organisation and Structure   **55**

3.1 Setting up a Town Council   55
3.2 Organisation and Structure of Town Council   60
3.3 Terms of Reference for Standing Committees   60
3.4 Town Council Meetings   64
3.5 Budgeting and Reports   65

Chapter 4 Routine Maintenance Management   **71**

4.1 Introduction   71
4.2 Types and Scope of Routine Maintenance Work   72
4.3 Term Contracts for Routine Maintenance Work   76
4.4 Maintenance Policies and By-laws   78
4.5 Estate Inspection System (EIS)   81
4.6 Integrated Estate Management System (IEMS)   82
4.7 Lift Dashboard Management System   86
4.8 Work Order System   88
4.9 Customer Service Delivery System   90
4.10 Management of Complex Problems   102
4.11 Resident Engagement and Public Relations   117

Chapter 5 Cyclical Maintenance Management   **119**

5.1 Introduction   119
5.2 Types of Cyclical Maintenance Work   121
5.3 Annual Planning of Cyclical Maintenance Work   123
5.4 Procurement of Cyclical Maintenance Work   124
5.5 Tendering Process for Cyclical Maintenance Work   125
5.6 Tender Evaluation Method   126

Chapter 6 Town Improvement Project Management   **129**

6.1 Town Council Plan   129
6.2 Common Town Improvement Projects   130
6.3 Stakeholders' Engagement and Professional Consultations   132
6.4 Understanding Users' Requirements   134
6.5 Town Identity and Branding   136

Chapter 7 Town Upgrading Programmes   **139**

    7.1 Introduction   139
    7.2 Key Estate Upgrading Programmes   142

Chapter 8 Business Continuity Management System and
               Future Challenges   **153**

    8.1 Introduction   153
    8.2 Business Continuity Management System (BCMS)   154
    8.3 Benefits of Business Continuity Management System   178
    8.4 Future Challenges   179

Index   183

Acknowledgements

Handbook of Township Management is the first comprehensive book written on public housing management in Singapore. I wish to express my deep gratitude and thanks to the People's Action Party (PAP) town councils for the encouragement and support over the years. In particular, I am grateful to my former parliamentary colleagues and town council general managers for sharing their best practices in township management when I was co-ordinating Chairman for the 15 PAP town councils. The collective wisdom of the town council chairmen and general managers have facilitated the compilation of policies, processes and effective solutions on township management in this book. I also wish to thank the various government agencies for their guidance and support to the town councils. The partnership and collaboration of government agencies and town councils have resulted in the implementation of many innovative projects that have benefitted our residents in the respective towns.

I wish to express my special thanks to the dedicated and helpful librarians at the Singapore Parliament Library for their assistance in my research on town councils. Many of my former town council colleagues and friends have also been forthcoming in sharing their knowledge and experiences with me. In particular, I would like to thank Soon Min Sin, Juliana Lim, Frank Ngoh, Lawrence Toh, Andrea Tay and Yang Mei Ling for their assistance and contributions. I also wish to thank Eugene Seah and Ervine Tan for sharing their experiences on the implementation of the Town Council's Integrated Estate Management System and Lift Telemonitoring System.

Finally, I wish to thank my family members for the support which they have given me. It has been a rewarding journey to run town councils, and I am honoured to be given the opportunity to serve my residents as town council chairman for 20 years.

Note from the Author

The opinions in the book are not representative of the government and its agencies (MND, HDB, etc.). Readers should check on latest information or data pertaining to Government schemes and programmes from official sources.

Preface

Singapore has implemented one of the most successful public housing programmes in the World. Over the last 60 years, the Housing and Development Board (HDB) of Singapore has built over one million public housing flats (HDB flats) to house 80% of Singaporeans. The key mission of HDB is to provide affordable, quality housing and a great living environment where communities thrive. In doing so, it has also won many international awards for its innovation, engineering excellence and sustainable business practices. As a developer, HDB continues its "after-sales" service and works closely with town councils to ensure that Singaporeans continue to enjoy a safe and quality living environment where they set up homes, form families and age in the community.

In 1988, the Singapore Parliament passed the Town Councils Act to form town councils. The purpose of setting up town councils is to encourage residents to take ownership in the running of their estates. The town councils also provide opportunities for the elected Members of Parliament (MPs) to better serve their residents in public housing estates. Based on the electoral boundaries of constituencies, elected MPs will either form their own towns or work with other MPs to form larger towns for management. The key role of the town council is to control, manage, maintain and improve the common property of HDB flats and estates.

This book is specially written based on the experience of the author who has been involved in town councils for over 30 years. Dr Teo started as a town council volunteer in 1991 and became the CEO of Jurong Town Council from 1992 to 1996. After being elected as an MP in 1996, he continued to serve the town councils. He was chairman of Holland-Bukit Panjang Town Council from 2001 to 2020 and coordinating chairman of 15 People's Action Party (PAP) town councils from 2006 to 2020.

Handbook of Township Management is a practice guide which highlights the key professional practices of township management in Singapore. It provides a comprehensive coverage of the purpose, setup, objectives, scope of work, processes and toolkits of town councils and incorporates case studies of complex problems faced by town councils. This book is based on the collective experiences of the town councils, and various best practices are highlighted to enable town councils to provide better services to serve HDB residents and stakeholders of HDB towns. The book also aims to uplift the professionalism of township management and facilities management in the built environment industry.

Chapter 1

Introduction of Town Council in Singapore

1.1 Public Housing in Singapore

The success of Singapore's public housing is attributed to its political leaders' visions, government policies, public housing development programmes and town council management. Over 80% of Singaporeans stay in public housing — also commonly known as Housing and Development Board (HDB) flats — in 17 towns, as demarcated by political electoral boundaries. After every parliamentary general election, elected Members of Parliament (MPs) gather and form their respective towns based on their electoral constituencies, which comprise Group Representation Constituencies (GRCs) and Single Member Constituencies (SMCs). Each town manages the HDB residential flats, HDB commercial shops and hawker stalls in their respective public housing estates. The size of a town may range from 40,000 to 100,000 residential and commercial units. The grouping of constituencies into towns provides economies of scale in the management of public housing estates. This also enables town councils to implement townwide improvement and upgrading projects to fulfil the needs and aspirations of their respective residents and stakeholders.

1.2 Concept of Town Council

Prior to the formation of the town council, public housing estates were managed and maintained by the HDB. As a statutory board, HDB implemented consistent housing policies and programmes across Singapore, and as a result, many estates look similar and can appear rather monotonous. Very often, residents did not have many opportunities to participate in the management and improvement of their estates. This lack of participation among the residents and stakeholders of a town sparked the idea of forming town councils so as to encourage residents to take ownership in the management of their estates. As such, the Town Councils Act stipulates that two-third of the town councillors in a town must comprise residents of the town. This composition of the town council would then provide more opportunities for residents, community leaders and various stakeholders of the town to be appointed to the decision-making body of the town.

With the participation of residents in town council management, the councils could then formulate policies and by-laws within the towns to better manage the estates to fulfil the needs and aspirations of their residents. The councils would also be empowered to develop a distinctive character and identity for their respective towns. This would then develop a greater sense of belonging and identity among residents and stakeholders of the respective towns. These arrangements would also complement the housing policies to promote home ownership among Singaporeans.

Thus, the concept of a town council — which involves the participation of both the elected MPs and residents in public housing management — aims to achieve the following objectives:

- Give the elected MPs the authority and responsibility to manage public housing estates in their constituencies.
- Ensure that the elected MPs are directly accountable to their constituents in the management of town councils.
- Encourage residents, stakeholders and volunteers to participate in the decision-making process of the town councils.
- Cultivate a sense of shared responsibility among residents and stakeholders in town council management.
- Allow each town to develop its own distinctive character and identity.
- Provide opportunities for elected MPs to lead the management, improvement and upgrading of their estates to enhance the quality of life of their constituents and gain political mileage.

1.3 Formation of Town Council

In 1988, the Singapore Parliament passed the Town Councils Act to form town councils. The key role of the town council is to control, manage, maintain and improve the common property of HDB flats and estates. The scope of work for the maintenance of common property includes the following:

- formulation of policies, by-laws and enforcement,
- cleaning services,
- building maintenance,
- mechanical and electrical maintenance,
- horticulture and landscaping maintenance,
- pest control work,
- estate improvement work,
- estate upgrading work,
- public relations work.

1.4 Purpose of Town Council

The purpose of the town council is to control, manage, maintain and improve the common property of housing estates of the HDB.

- **Control**: This refers to the control of the use of common property, activities and user behaviour in the town. The town council will implement policies and by-laws to control the use of common property, and manage anti-social behaviour such as littering, vandalism, nuisance, obstructions and actions which pose safety hazards to others in the estates (e.g. throwing high-rise killer litter, reckless riding of motorbikes, bicycles or personal mobility devices, and placing combustible materials at common properties). The council may issue a permit or Temporary Occupation Licence (TOL) for the use of common property and authorise installations, such as signages, awnings, or kiosks.
- **Manage**: This refers to the overall strategic and facilities management of the town, such as the development of long-term (5-year Master Plan) and short-term (Annual Work Plan) plans for the town. The management

function entails taking over new HDB flats for management from HDB, managing the common property of existing residential and commercial property, and handing over or taking over flats after every parliamentary general election or by-election due to the formation of new towns.

- **Maintain**: This refers to the maintenance and repair of common property of residential and commercial property of HDB estates and keeping them in a state of good and serviceable repair and in a proper and clean condition. These works include inspection of estates, cleaning, grass-cutting and landscaping works, servicing of mechanical and electrical installations, management of complaints and feedback, and general repairs.
- **Improve**: This refers to the implementation of improvement projects to enhance the living environment and fulfill the rising aspirations of residents. Improvement projects such as covered linkways, children's playgrounds, fitness corners, community halls and multi-purpose courts will provide more convenience to residents and facilitate the building of community bonds. Improvement works also include lift upgrading programme and estate renewal programme, including the revitalisation of HDB commercial shops.

1.5 Key Stakeholders of Town Council

Figure 1.1 shows the key stakeholders of a town council. As a corporate entity empowered to perform various functions in the management of a town, it is essential for the town council to understand the profile, needs, requirements, and aspirations of its key stakeholders. The key stakeholders of a town are as follows:

- elected MPs,
- appointed town councillors,
- grassroots organisations/grassroots leaders,
- HDB residents,
- HDB shop owners/tenants,
- HDB hawker stallholders,
- government agencies,

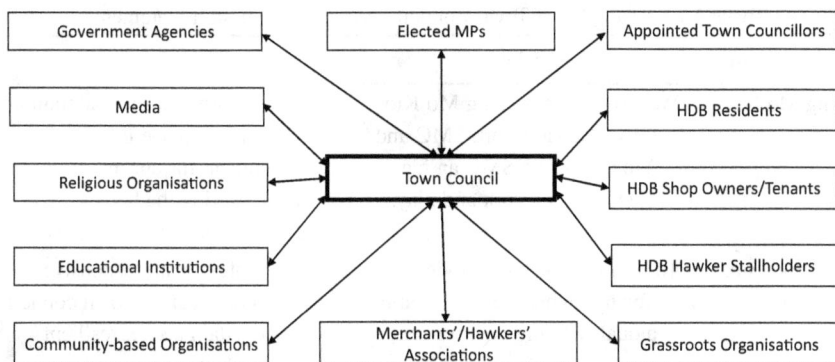

Figure 1.1 Key Stakeholders of Town Council

- community-based organisations,
- educational institutions,
- religious institutions,
- merchants'/hawkers' associations,
- media.

  - **Elected MPs**: The MPs are responsible for running the town councils and managing the HDB estates to serve their residents. Due to the different profiles of residents in different towns, MPs from different town councils will have different visions and motivations to develop unique characteristics for their respective towns. Examples of town councils' vision and mission statements are shown in Table 1.1.
  - **Appointed town councillors**: Appointed Town Councillors are volunteers who contribute their expertise, time and resources to the management of a town. They play a key role in ensuring good corporate governance and providing important linkages between the town council and its stakeholders. The appointed councillors can come from different backgrounds, such as the professional, business, community or public sectors. Their collective expertise and experience will help the town councils be more innovative in enhancing the living environment to better serve their residents.
  - **Grassroots organisations/grassroots leaders**: Grassroots organisations and grassroots leaders are key partners as they are the

Table 1.1   Examples of Town Council's Vision and Mission Statements

Town Council	Vision	Mission
Ang Mo Kio	We strive to make Ang Mo Kio GRC, Kebun Bahru SMC and Yio Chu Kang SMC an ideal place to live, work and play.	We want to provide and maintain a safe and conducive living environment for our residents while ensuring the highest level of service and professionalism.
Holland-Bukit Panjang	To be a sustainable and vibrant Town in which residents enjoy a quality living environment.	To be a professional, responsive and resident-centric town council so as to attain a safe, resilient and sustainable town and encourage ownership among residents.
Nee Soon	Home with a heart.	Building a safe, inclusive, sustainable and vibrant town.
Tampines	"Tampines Together" is to develop a community that is actively engaged in five core areas: 1. Learning 2. Green 3. Active 4. Caring 5. Creative For a greater sense of belonging, building stronger ties, lead a more enticing life, stay healthy and together, Make Tampines Our Best Home.	To make Tampines truly our best home where we live, work, play, bring up our children and grow old in peace, comfort and harmony.
Tanjong Pagar	To build a caring, sustainable and connected community.	To provide high quality living environment for the HDB residents in Tanjong Pagar Town.
Sembawang	Building a resident-centric Sembawang Town based on excellence of its people, its facilities, services and attractions.	Encouraging active participation of our residents in the management of the town to improve our facilities, services to make Sembawang Town a more attractive place to live in.

"mouths and ears" of town councils. They are familiar with the residents' needs and aspirations, and thus can provide invaluable feedback to town councils to improve the quality of services and add amenities which will in turn improve the living environment for the residents. The town councils will usually engage the Citizens' Consultative Committee (CCC) and Residents' Committee (RC) or Residents' Network (RN) of their respective towns on matters such as residents' consultations (surveys and town hall meetings), updates on routine and cyclical maintenance works, and progress reports on improvement and upgrading projects.

- **HDB residents**: HDB residents are key stakeholders of a town. They pay monthly service and conservancy charges for the provision of maintenance services by town councils. As such, different residents would have different expectations of the quality of services and improvement works provided by the town councils. Depending on the age profile of residents, flat types (1, 2, 3, 4, 5 rooms or executive flats) and interests of the residents, their needs and expectations can vary from town to town or among neighbouring estates within the town. Younger families in new towns will usually need more child-friendly amenities while matured towns with an ageing population will require more senior-friendly facilities.

- **HDB shop owners/tenants**: HDB commercial shops are usually located in town centres and neighbourhood centres to provide a range of goods and services for residents. Some shops were sold by HDB and owned by shop owners who may operate or rent out their shops while the rest are rental shops from HDB. Due to the trade mix of shops, different shop operators will have different needs and requirements for their businesses. In some towns, the shop owners/operators may form merchants' associations to take care of their collective interests. Some shop owners or operators are also grassroots leaders and/or town councilors and can provide useful linkages for town councils to develop partnerships with the merchants' associations.

- **HDB hawker stallholders**: Hawker stallholders are usually located in wet markets and hawker centres in different parts of the towns. They operate at different hours of the day based on the needs of their customers, and they tend to get busier during weekends and festive seasons, such as Chinese New Year, Qingming festival, Hari Raya celebrations, Deepavali, Christmas, and New Year. Similarly, hawkers may gather to form hawkers' association to take care of their collective interests and some of them are grassroots leaders and/or town councillors.

- **Government agencies**: As required by the Town Councils Act, the town councils must collaborate with various government agencies for the benefit of the residents. The town councils will engage and work closely with various government agencies, such as the Housing and Development Board (HDB), National Environment Agency (NEA), Municipal Services Office (MSO), Land Transport Authority (LTA), Public Utilities Board (PUB), Singapore Police Force (SPF), Singapore Civil Defence Force (SCDF), Building and Construction Authority (BCA), National Parks Board (NParks), Urban Redevelopment Authority of Singapore (URA), and relevant ministries. Besides compliance with the various regulations of the authorities, the town councils may partner with the government agencies to implement projects or programmes such as the HDB neighbourhood renewal programme, landscaping of town, rat attack programme, covered linkways to transport nodes, and neighbourhood safety and security initiatives.
- **Community-based organisations**: There are many community partners which town councils engage and collaborate with in the management of a town. These community-based organisations include social service agencies, non-government organisations, trade associations, and professional bodies. Very often, the town councils will partner with these organisations to resolve municipal problems or issues, such as neighbour disputes, animal nuisance, religious frictions, welfare assistance programs or corporate social responsibility projects.
- **Educational institutions**: The town councils also partner with schools and educational institutions to implement various town council activities, such as town day, tree planting, green projects or campaigns to promote gracious and green living in the town.
- **Religious organisations**: There are many religious organisations located within a town as Singapore is a multi-racial and

multi-religious society. Chinese temples, mosques, Indian temples, churches and other places of worship are usually built within the housing estates for the convenience for the residents. Due to the different religious practices, the town councils have to work closely with various religious organisations to educate and seek mutual understanding among residents regarding religious matters.

- **Merchants'/hawkers' associations**: Shop owners and hawker stallholders within a precinct or town can form merchants' or hawkers' associations to represent their collective interests when engaging the town councils or government agencies. These associations are usually run by volunteers who are representatives of the shops or hawker stalls. Due to the tenant mix of shops and hawker stalls, the requirements of the merchants' and hawkers' associations vary in different precincts and towns. Common issues faced by shops and hawkers include the display of goods at common areas, pest control issues, cleaning and conservancy matters, enforcement by town councils or government agencies, and upgrading of neighbourhood and town centres.
- **Media**: The media and social media play an important role in facilitating the work of the town council. Good and bad news can be featured or go viral on social media, thus affecting the image of the town council. Thus, it is crucial for the town council to adopt an appropriate media and social media engagement strategy to achieve a win-win outcome for the reporting of town councils' happenings. Different media and social media platforms have different target audiences. As such, the town councils must utilise these media and social media platforms to inform and educate the residents and stakeholders. At the same time, these messages from town councils will help to profile and brand the town.

1.6 Desired Outcomes of Town Council Management

Based on the vision and mission of the town councils, the councils will then identify the key desired outcomes to guide the management and

ensure good corporate governance of the council. The key desired outcomes of township management are as follows:

(a) well-maintained estates;
(b) better facilities and amenities;
(c) good customer service delivery;
(d) safe and secure estates;
(e) clean and green environment;
(f) good financial health;
(g) good corporate governance;
(h) good image and branding;
(i) strong partnership among stakeholders; and
(j) happy and supportive residents and stakeholders.

- **Well-maintained estates**: The key duties of the town council are
  to control, manage, maintain, and improve the common property of
  the residential and commercial property in HDB estates. According
  to Section 23 of the Town Councils Act, the common property must
  be maintained and kept "in a state of good and serviceable repair"
  condition. As the supervising ministry, the Ministry of National
  Development will conduct regular inspections to check on the state
  of cleanliness and maintenance of every town. It will also provide
  an annual Town Council Management Report (TCMR) to each town
  council as feedback to further improve the services provided by
  town councils to its residents.
- **Better facilities and amenities**: To fulfil the needs and aspirations
  of the residents, the town council must engage its stakeholders and
  improve the facilities and amenities in the town. The town council shall provide professional services and exercise due diligence
  when implementing town improvement projects and upgrading
  programmes. This entails the engagement of the relevant stakeholders for different improvement and upgrading projects. The understanding of stakeholders' requirements will ensure that the projects
  implemented can better meet the needs and expectations of residents and stakeholders.
- **Good customer service delivery**: The town council should strive
  to give residents and stakeholders a positive experience when

providing services to them. It shall also develop a good customer service framework and culture to continuously improve its services to residents and stakeholders. Good customer service entails prompt response and effective resolution of problems, and this will build trust in the town council and encourage residents to rely on it. The town council must also conduct regular customer service surveys to monitor and improve its service delivery.

- **Safe and secure estates**: The estates must be maintained to ensure that they are safe for their residents and stakeholders, especially senior citizens and children. Residents must feel safe to move around freely in the town during the day and night. Appropriate workplace and safety health measures must be implemented to keep the workers and the public safe. At the same time, the use of technology and community participation will further strengthen the safety and security of the estates, and these can take the form of closed-circuit televisions (CCTVs) or community watch groups.
- **Clean and green environment**: The adoption of sustainable practices in town council operations will ensure a clean and green living environment for the residents and stakeholders. Providing "green lungs" and implementing green projects will further improve the built environment of the town. Environmental education of residents will promote a green lifestyle and build a green culture among residents. The town councils may wish to adopt the Environmental, Social and Governance (ESG) framework to implement sustainable development and promote a green culture among residents and stakeholders in the town.
- **Good financial health**: Financial prudence and due diligence must be exercised to ensure that town council funds are properly received and expended in accordance with the Town Councils Act and Town Councils Financial Rules. This includes the investment of town council funds to attain healthy returns and the management of arrears in service and conservancy charges collection.
- **Good corporate governance**: A robust checks and balances internal control system must be set up to ensure compliance with the Town Councils Act, Town Councils Financial Rules, and Code of Corporate Governance. Professional Code of Ethics must be

practised in the engagement of stakeholders and delivery of town council services. Due diligence must be exercised in the management of town council funds to ensure public accountability.

- **Good image and branding**: A good image for the town that is in line with its vision and mission. The town has developed a unique character and identity which promotes ownership and a sense of belonging among residents and its stakeholders. The elected MPs gain political mileage in running a successful town.
- **Strong partnership among stakeholders**: Stakeholders are working in close partnership with the town council to better serve the residents. Strong and sustained partnership further improves the quality of town council services to better meet the needs of residents and stakeholders.
- **Happy and supportive residents and stakeholders**: It is important for residents and stakeholders to feel appreciative and happy with the services of the town council. All residents and stakeholders need to be engaged and kept updated on the development and activities of the town. Results of customer satisfaction surveys which are encouraging and positive would reflect strong support for the town council and its elected MPs.

1.7 Key Business Functions of Town Council Management

As stated in Section 20 of the Town Councils Act, the functions of the town council are as follows:

- To control, manage, maintain and improve the common property of the residential and commercial property in the housing estates of the board within the town for the benefit of the residents of those housing estates and to keep them in a state of good and serviceable repair and in a proper and clean condition; and
- To exercise such powers and perform such duties as may from time to time be conferred or imposed on the town council by or under this Act.

The "common property" of residential and commercial property in HDB estates is defined by Section 2 of the Town Councils Act to include the following:

- the columns, beams, supports, external walls, roofs and storage spaces, lobbies, corridors, stairs, stairways, fire escapes, entrances and exits;
- firefighting and protection system;
- the central and appurtenant installations for services such as power, light, sanitation and water;
- the escalators, lifts, water tanks, pumps, motors, fans, compressors, ducts and all other apparatus and installations existing for common use;
- the common facilities in the housing estates built for the use or enjoyment of the residents;
- all recreational or community facilities, and gardens;
- all directional signs and signboards;
- all land appurtenant to the building and all other parts of the land intended for the use or enjoyment of the residents;
- such other property as may be prescribed,

but does not include the following:

- bus terminals and interchanges;
- drains, sewers and lightings maintained by the government;
- swimming pools and other sports complexes;
- public roads and parking places;
- such other property as may be prescribed.

One key aspect to understand about town council management is that the town council is only responsible for the management of common property of the residential and commercial property in the HDB estates. Thus, private estates and other properties in the town do not come under the jurisdiction of the town council. Very often, residents and stakeholders are confused as to which agency to provide feedback to when they face various municipal issues in their estates. This is due to the different ownership of property and land in the estates such as private landowners, public land and properties managed by various ministries and government agencies, such as the Singapore Land Authority, Public Utilities Board, or Land Transport Authority.

To overcome this confusion and adopt a "no wrong door" policy, the government has set up the Municipal Services Office (MSO) to help coordinate all feedback on issues pertaining to 10 government agencies. A mobile application (One Service Mobile App) was developed to receive feedback on municipal issues and ensure follow-up actions are taken by the relevant agencies. This has improved the resolution rate of municipal issues over the years.

The key business functions of a town council include the following:

(a) secretariat, administrative and compliance services;
(b) accounting services and financial management;
(c) routine maintenance management;
(d) cyclical maintenance management;
(e) improvement projects and upgrading programme management;
(f) contracts and project management;
(g) stakeholder engagement and public relations; and
(h) business continuity management.

- **Secretariat, administrative & compliance services**: This entails the administrative support provided by the managing agent staff or town council staff to ensure the smooth running of the day-to-day operations of the town council. It includes the setting up of town councils after every parliamentary general election or by-election, appointing a managing agent and/or recruitment of staff, submissions to the ministry and gazetting of town council information for public scrutiny, managing the front-end reception and customer service call centre, providing secretariat support to town council meetings, and compliance with the Town Councils Act, Town Councils Financial Rules, Town Council By-laws, and relevant legislations.
- **Accounting services and financial management**: This entails the setting up of separate funds (operating and sinking funds) for town council and the keeping of proper accounts and records of

the transactions and affairs of the town council. It includes annual budgeting, collection of service and conservancy charges, and other collectibles, payment of expenses, and investment of town council funds. In addition, the council must set up internal control mechanisms to ensure checks and balances in the management of risks in its operations. All transactions shall adhere strictly to the Town Councils Act and Town Councils Financial Rules. The audited accounts and annual report shall be submitted to the ministry and parliament for public accountability purposes annually.

- **Routine maintenance management**: This entails the planning and execution of routine maintenance works to ensure that the estates are kept in clean, proper and serviceable conditions. It includes planning and conducting estate inspections, and the management of term contractors to carry out works, such as cleaning, repairs, horticultural landscaping and grass-cutting, servicing of mechanical and electrical installations, pest control works and management of common property in the town. These works are usually carried out on a daily, weekly, bi-monthly, monthly, quarterly or yearly basis depending on the recommended frequency of maintenance by manufacturers, statutory requirements and user requirements. Routine maintenance also involves the management of feedback and complaints received from residents and stakeholders for the purpose of delivering great customer service. Expenditure for routine maintenance work is usually planned on an annual basis using the town council's operating fund.

- **Cyclical maintenance management**: This entails the planning and execution of maintenance works which are cyclical in nature to renew or replace building components and elements. The frequency of cyclical maintenance work is based on the life cycle schedule as recommended by the ministry or the manufacturers. It includes the renewal or replacement of building components and elements, electrical system, water and sanitation system, lift and escalator system, fire protection system, waste management system and alarm alert system. Expenditure for cyclical maintenance work is usually planned on a 10-year work plan using the town council's sinking funds.

- **Improvement projects and upgrading programmes management**: This entails the implementation of improvement projects and estate upgrading programmes to enhance the living environment of the residents. Improvement projects are normally carried out based on the needs and aspirations of the residents. There are various channels through which the town council will receive feedback and suggestions from residents and stakeholders. Depending on the types of improvement projects, the town council will engage and consult residents and stakeholders to ensure that these projects can better meet their needs and expectations. In addition, the HDB will also implement upgrading programmes to rejuvenate older housing estates, such as the Neighbourhood Renewal Programme (NRP), Lift Upgrading Programme (LUP), Home Improvement Programme (HIP) and Revitalisation of Shops scheme (ROS). The town council plays a key role in the implementation of both improvement projects and upgrading programmes in the town.
- **Contracts and project management**: This entails the preparation and procurement of contracts for routine maintenance works, cyclical maintenance works, improvement projects and upgrading programmes for the town. The town council will consult different stakeholders to identify the requirements of a project and prepare the tender specifications for the calling of tenders according to the Town Council Financial Rules. Very often, tender bids submitted will be evaluated based on the Price Quality Method (PQM), which focuses on the competitive pricing and track records of quality performance of the bidders. Once the contract is awarded, the project management team will proceed to manage the project to achieve the time, cost, quality and safety objectives of the project. The purpose of this is to ensure that the town council complies with the Town Councils Act and Town Councils Financial Rules in selecting suitable contractors to complete projects successfully, so that town councils can be accountable to the public and that the contractors offering the best value proposition are selected.
- **Stakeholder engagement and public relations**: This entails the engagement of different stakeholders so as to build rapport and good relations in achieving the vision and mission of the town coun-

cil. The town council will inform, consult and engage residents and stakeholders so as to ensure better fulfilment of their needs and aspirations. At the same time, the town council will promote a greater sense of belonging by getting residents involved in the management of the town. Public relations with stakeholders and media (including social media) plays an important part in developing town identity and promoting ownership among residents.

- **Business continuity management**: This entails the development of Business Continuity Plans (BCPs) to ensure that town council operations are not disrupted by natural or man-made disasters, such as disease outbreaks, extreme weather conditions, terrorist attacks, fires, cyberattacks, and power outages. It involves identifying these risks and analysing their impact on key business operations so that response, recovery and resilient measures can be planned and implemented. As town councils provide essential services to ensure the health and safety of residents in the HDB estates, it is crucial to develop business continuity plans and conduct regular exercises so that the town council teams can respond to these disasters more effectively.

1.8 Key Performance Indicators of Town Council Management

Over the years, the government and town councils have developed various mechanisms to measure the performance of town councils. This is to ensure that town councils are properly managed in accordance with the Town Councils Act, Town Councils Financial Rules, and Town Council Code of Governance. The key performance indicators of town councils are listed as follows:

(a) Town Council Management Report (assessment by MND);
(b) Internal and External Auditors' Reports;
(c) Integrated Estate Management System Report;
(d) Lift Performance Management System Report;
(e) Customer Service Delivery Survey;

(f) Sustainability Report; and

(g) Town Council Annual Report (presented to the Singapore Parliament).

- **Town Council Management Report (TCMR)**: The Town Council Management Report was introduced by the Ministry of National Development to provide a framework for measuring the performance of town councils. It sets out performance indicators and measures the achievements of town councils in five key areas: (a) estate cleanliness, (b) estate maintenance, (c) lift performance, (d) service and conservancy charges arrears management, and (e) corporate governance. Random inspection of the estates is carried out by the ministry on a monthly basis and the TCMR will be conveyed yearly to the respective town councils for their reference and further action. The TCMR provides an overall benchmarking of the performance of all town councils.

- **Internal and External Auditors' Reports**: The town council will engage internal and external auditors to audit its financial statements and internal control measures for financial management and corporate governance purposes. The external auditors will conduct a financial audit and prepare a statement for submission to the ministry and parliament, while the internal auditors will ensure that checks and balances are in place to ensure good corporate governance of the town council.

- **Integrated Estate Management System (IEMS) Report**: The IEMS provides operational reports to ensure that feedback is properly registered in the system and follow-up actions are taken. It is a centralised computerised system to capture data on residents' and stakeholders' feedback regarding all town council and municipal issues. Data analytics and dashboard systems are set up to support the town council management team and improve its service delivery. The IEMS is also linked to the Municipal Services Office (MSO) One Service App which receives feedback on municipal issues for 10 other government agencies. Thus, the IEMS and One Service App provide a one-stop service (i.e. "no wrong door" policy) for residents and stakeholders to provide feedback on all municipal issues, such as urban planning, town council, housing, construction, transport, utilities, environment, safety, security and community.

- **Lift Performance Management Report**: The lift performance management report provides information to monitor the performance of the lifts and lift contractors. Operational reports will highlight the breakdown rate, lift downtime, and operational status of lifts in different estates in the town according to lift types and companies. Historical trends analysis and maintenance records will further help the town council enhance the overall performance of lifts. A lift dashboard management system is set up to monitor all lifts so that town council can respond promptly to reduce the downtime of lifts. This ensures better performance and reliability of the lifts, thus providing convenience to residents.
- **Customer Service Delivery Survey**: Town council will normally conduct a customer service delivery survey yearly or on a needs basis to gather feedback on the quality of services and the satisfaction of its residents and stakeholders. The survey will assess the effectiveness of town council services in various areas such as reception service, payment service, call centre service, property management service and improvement projects. The survey is usually outsourced to an independent organisation or firm and conducted using random sampling.
- **Sustainability Report**: Town council will also publish its sustainability report on a voluntary basis to highlight its ESG efforts that were undertaken to ameliorate the effects of climate change. Some town councils will also have master plans relating to the sustainable development of their towns. The master plans will highlight key performance indicators to determine if such ESG efforts have been successfully implemented. The sustainability report provides a framework and platform for town council to better engage its stakeholders to promote sustainability in township management.
- **Town Council Annual Report**: As required by the Town Councils Act, every town council must submit an annual report with its audited financial statement to the Ministry of National Development and Parliament. This is to ensure good corporate governance and public accountability as town councils are entrusted with significant amounts of public funds. The town council annual report is available for public scrutiny in the Singapore Parliament. The annual

report is also posted on the town council website for residents and stakeholders.

1.9 Proceedings of Town Council

Section 39 of the Town Councils Act states that: "A Town Council may make standing orders for regulating its procedure and, in particular, the standing orders may make such provision for the preservation of order at meetings as the Town Council may consider necessary." The standing order can include the formation of standing committees, frequency of meetings and quorum, and delegation of powers. Proper minutes of meetings shall be kept for both council and committee meetings. Decision-making shall be made based on votes from a simple majority of members present. The minimum quorum of any meeting of a town council shall be one-third of the number of members. The quorum for committee meetings shall be based on standing order provisions. A typical Standing Order of a town council is shown in Table 1.2.

Table 1.2　Standing Order of a Town Council

A. Meetings of the Town Council and Its Committees		
1　Preamble	1.1	These orders are cited as the Standing Orders for the Town Council.
2　Types of Meetings	2.1	The Town Council shall hold its meetings on the 4th Tuesday of the month or on a date decided by the Chairperson, subject to Standing Orders 2.2 and 2.3.
	2.2	The Chairperson may at any time summon a meeting of the Town Council.
	2.3	The Chairperson shall, on a requisition signed by not less than two-thirds of the members of the Town Council to that effect, summon a meeting of the Town Council within 7 days of receiving the requisition.
3.　Frequency of Meetings	3.1	The Town Council shall hold its meeting at least once every two months during its term. The Executive Committee shall meet as and when necessary in lieu of the Town Council.
	3.2	Every standing committee shall meet every two months except in an emergency or in need to implement policies affecting the Town Council and its residents.

Table 1.2   (*Continued*)

4.	Notice of Meetings	4.1	Notice of a meeting shall be given by the Secretary to each member of the Town Council at least 2 working days before the day of each meeting, except in the case of emergency meeting when as long a notice as possible shall be given.
			Such a notice may be transmitted by hand, post, or email.
		4.2	The notice of meeting shall include, if possible:
			(a) the agenda as well as relevant minutes, notes and information to enable Members of the Town Council to make preparation for discussion of the items enumerated there in;
			(b) subject to Standing Order 8.3, a copy of each proposed Motion and/or Resolution or any other matter to be considered at the meeting; and
			(c) details of the date, time and place of the meeting.
5.	Attendance	5.1	Every member of the Town Council is expected to attend and participate at the meetings.
		5.2	Members intending to be absent from Singapore for any period beyond 1 month, shall endeavour to keep the Secretary of the Town Council informed.
		5.3	Any appointed member who is absent without the leave of the Chairperson for three consecutive meetings shall vacate his or her office.
6.	Quorum for Meeting	6.1	No business shall be transacted at any meeting of the Town Council or any Committee unless a quorum is present at the commencement of the meeting.
		6.2	The quorum for any meeting of the Town Council shall be one-third of the total number of members.
		6.3	The quorum for any meeting of the standing committee shall be half of the total number of members.
7.	Procedures of Meeting	7.1	The Chairperson of the Town Council and each Committee shall preside at meetings.
			In the absence of the Chairperson, the Vice-Chairperson shall preside at the meeting.
			If both the Chairperson and the Vice-Chairperson are absent from a meeting, the members present at the meeting shall elect from among themselves a temporary Chairperson to preside at the meeting.
			The meetings of the Town Council shall be conducted in the following order:

(*Continued*)

Table 1.2   (*Continued*)

		(a) the Chairperson shall authenticate the minutes of the previous meeting in accordance with the provisions stipulated in Standing Order 13.1 herein; (b) the matters, if any, arising from the minutes of the previous meeting shall be discussed; and (c) thereafter, items on the agenda of the meeting shall be discussed in the order in which they are enumerated.
8.	Motion	8.1 A Motion is a proposal relating to an item of business for which a decision at the meeting is to be taken.
		8.2 Notwithstanding Standing Order 4.2(a), a Motion which has not been included in the Notice of meeting may be raised in the meeting, with leave of the Chairperson.
		8.3 The Chairperson may rule that a Motion submitted at the meeting is out of order if he or she considers that the Motion if carried, would be in breach of the Town Councils Act or its by-laws or would otherwise be unlawful or unenforceable.
		8.4 The Member moving the Motion shall have the right to speak first and again at the end, restricting himself or herself to points raised by other members.
		8.5 The Chairperson may bring the debate to an end by calling the proposer to reply and put the matter to the Council for decision.
9.	Resolutions	9.1 A Motion which is passed at the meeting by a simple majority of the members present becomes a Resolution.
10.	Voting and Circulation of Papers	10.1 All issues coming or arising before a Meeting of the Town Council or any of its Committees shall be decided by a simple majority of the members present and voting by a show of hands or otherwise as the Chairperson may direct.
		10.2 At any meeting of a Town Council or any of its Committees, the Chairperson or other person presiding shall have an original vote and also, if the votes are equal, a casting vote.
		10.3 The Town Council or any Committee may determine any matter by circulating papers.
		10.4 If any member does not notify the Council within the specified time that he or she disagrees with any matter in the paper, it is assumed that he or she agrees to it.

Table 1.2 (*Continued*)

11. Disclosure of Interest	11.1	As soon as any member becomes aware of a conflict of interest in a question that has arisen or is about to arise before the Town Council, the member must disclose in writing the fact, nature, character and extent of the personal or financial interest that gives rise to the conflict to the Secretary and to the Chairperson.
	11.2	Any member who is in any way, directly or indirectly, interested in a transaction or project of the Town Council must disclose his or her interest at the Town Council Meeting. The disclosure must be recorded in the minutes accordingly.
	11.3	For the purpose of determining the quorum, such member shall be treated as being present in the Meeting but he or she must not take part or vote in any deliberation regarding the transaction or project.

B.   Keeping of Minutes and Records

12. Recording Minutes	12.1	Minutes of the proceedings of the Town Council and its Committees shall be kept in a permanent form and authenticated in accordance with the Standing Orders. The minutes shall include amongst other things, the following:
		(a) the nature and type of meeting;
		(b) the date, time and place at which the meeting was held;
		(c) the persons who constituted the meeting, i.e. the names of all present at the meeting and in what capacity they are attending the meeting;
		(d) records of Resolutions passed and all disclosures made by members in accordance to Standing Order 11.1;
		(e) records of the subject matter if financial and contractual transactions were considered during the meeting; and
		(f) records of all other specific businesses upon which decisions were taken.
13. Confirmation of Minutes	13.1	Minutes of each meeting shall be confirmed by members present at the next meeting and signed by the Chairperson.

(*Continued*)

Table 1.2 (*Continued*)

C. Appointment of Committees	
14. Standing Committees	14.1 Committees shall be appointed for specific purposes to better regulate and manage the Council matters. At least half of the members of each committee shall be members of the Town Council, one of whom will be elected as Chairperson of the committee. The following are the committees appointed:
	(a) Audit Committee
	(b) Contracts Committee
	(c) Estate Committee
	(d) Finance Committee
	(e) Project Committee
	(f) Publicity Committee

D. Others

15. Conduct	15.1 Town Councillors are committed to the prevention of harassment. Any harassment, whether verbal, physical or visual is not acceptable.
	15.2 Town Councillors are expected to conduct themselves in a proper manner befitting the role and office of the Town Council and to discharge their duties with integrity and to the best of their ability in a professional manner.
	15.3 Town Councillor shall declare to the Town Council Chairperson and Secretary if he or she:
	(a) ceases to be a citizen of Singapore;
	(b) becomes an undischarged bankrupt or has made any arrangement with his or her creditors; and
	(c) has been sentenced to imprisonment for a term of not less than one year or to a fine of not less than $2,000 and has not received a free pardon.
	15.4 Town Councillor shall update the Town Council Secretary if his or her official place of residence has changed.
16. Safeguard of Information, Intellectual Property and Assets	16.1 Town Councillors may be provided with sensitive or confidential information (including personal data) during the course of their work for the Town Council. Each Town Councillor shall not at any time during the continuance of or after their tenure, divulge either directly or indirectly to any person or company,

Table 1.2 (*Continued*)

	any knowledge or information which he or she may acquire during the course of or incidental to his or her tenure nor shall he or she use any such knowledge or information to advance his or her personal interest or the interests of his or her spouse, relative, friend or business partner.
	16.2 Town Councillors shall not speak with or be interviewed by the press or other media except with the prior consent of the Town Council Chairperson.
17. Gifts, Entertainment, Donations and Sponsorship	17.1 Town Councillors shall not at any time, accept any gifts from any contractor, vendor, supplier, business associate or member of public whom he or she comes into contact with in the course of his or her tenure. Gifts must be refused and returned, and if the circumstances do not allow the refusal or return, these gifts must be declared in writing to the Town Council Secretary. Gifts shall include but are not restricted to any festive hampers or other consumables and extraordinary discounts on purchases and services that are offered free of charge.
	17.2 Town Councillors shall not accept any invitation to receive entertainment from any contractor, vendor, supplier, business associate or member of public whom he or she comes into contact with in the course of his or her tenure. Entertainment shall include but are not restricted to free trips, airline tickets, hotel accommodation, karaoke, drinks, etc.
	17.3 Town Councillors shall not solicit any loans or business from any contractor, vendor, supplier, business associate or member of public whom he or she comes into contact with in the course of his or her tenure. This includes soliciting on behalf of his or her spouse, relatives, friends or business partners, or making any introduction for the purpose of a spouse, relative, friend or business partner to so solicit.
	17.4 Town Councillors shall not solicit any donations or sponsorships for their own personal benefit or for the benefit of their spouse, relative, friend or business partner.

(*Continued*)

Table 1.2   (*Continued*)

18. Return of Assets and Settlement of Payments	18.1	Town Councillors shall upon cessation of their tenure, immediately return to the Town Council all property and assets belonging to Town Council which may be in his or her possession or under his or her control.
	18.2	Town Councillors shall upon cessation of their tenure, immediately settle all outstanding payments and arrears due to the Town Council. These may include but are not restricted to allowances, authorized deductions, loans, unreturned assets, telecommunication and utilities bills, etc.
19. Asking Questions and Reporting	19.1	Town Councillors must be on the alert for any breach or potential breach of any Codes, Laws, Rules and Regulations. Any breach or suspected breach of such Codes, Laws, Rules and Regulations shall be reported to the Town Council Chairperson, Vice-Chairperson or Secretary.

Chapter 2

Town Council Governance

2.1 Introduction

As town councils manage over S$2 billion worth of public and residents' monies, the town councils are accountable to the public in their allocation of funds in running the town councils. Thus, the town councils must have a good corporate governance framework to ensure transparency and accountability to their residents and the general public. To attain good corporate governance, the town council must comply with the Town Councils Act and its subsidiary legislations (Town Councils Financial Rules). In addition, it has to adhere to the directives of all government agencies when carrying out its duties. The ministry and town councils have also worked together to develop a code of governance to complement the existing legislative framework. This code sets out the principles of good corporate governance and highlights best practices to guide town councils in executing their fiduciary responsibilities and public accountability.

2.2 Town Councils Act

The Town Councils Bill was passed in Parliament on 29 June 1988 (third reading of the bill) and the Town Councils Act commenced on 5 August 1988. The key provisions of the Act are as follows:

Part 1 of the Town Councils Act (Sections 1–3) defines certain terms in the act and provides the power for the Minister to declare an area to be a town. Definitions for a town, town council, constituency, town council chairperson, elected members, appointed members, key officers of town council and common property in relation to HDB residential and commercial property are set out to facilitate compliance with the Act.

Part 2 of the Town Councils Act (Sections 4–12) makes provisions for the establishment of a town council which shall consist of all elected Members of Parliament (MPs) for the constituencies comprised within the town. It also sets out the duties of town council chairperson and vice-chairpersons. The chairperson of the town council shall appoint town councillors of whom at least two-thirds shall be residents of the town.

Part 3 of the Town Councils Act (Section 13–19) states the tenure for both elected and appointed members of the town council. An MP shall be an elected member of the town council and shall only cease to be a member when he or she vacates his or her seat in Parliament. The chairperson and members of the council may be paid an allowance or salary out of the Town Council Fund.

Part 4 of the Town Councils Act (Sections 20–28) sets out the functions, powers, and duties of a town council. It empowers the Minister to direct the town council to take emergency-related measures for specific purposes. The council may also make by-laws for regulating the control, management, administration, use and enjoyment of the common property of the residential and commercial property in the HDB housing estates within the town.

Part 4A of the Town Councils Act (Sections 29–38) empowers the town council to carry out lift upgrading works within its respective towns, provided that at least 75% of the total voting value of votes of owners of the selected flats support the proposal at a poll.

Part 5 of the Town Councils Act (Sections 39–46) deals with the proceedings of a town council. A town council may make standing orders to determine its meeting procedures and frequency. It can appoint committees to carry out its functions under the act. It may also delegate its powers, functions and duties to its committees, employees, and agents. Decisions at meetings shall be based on a simple majority of the members present and voting.

Part 6 of the Town Councils Act (Sections 47–57) sets out the financial provisions relating to a town council. A town council shall establish separate funds for the maintenance of residential property, commercial property, and market and food centres. A town council is required to prepare annual accounts at the end of each financial year and the accounts shall be audited by the Auditor-General or such other auditor as may be appointed by the Minister in consultation with the Auditor-General. The audited financial statements, auditors' report and annual report of a town council shall be presented to Parliament.

Part 6A of the Town Councils Act (Sections 58–65) empowers the Minister to develop a plan or strategy for reviewing town councils so as to ensure that town councils conduct their business in accordance with the Town Councils Act.

Part 7 of the Town Councils Act (Sections 66–83) makes provisions for general and miscellaneous matters, such as recovery of arrears for conservancy and service charges, small claims tribunal proceedings and dissolution of a town council.

Figure 2.1 shows the steps involved in the establishment of a town council. After every parliamentary general election or by-election, the elected MPs will come together to form their towns based on their respective electoral boundaries. Among them, they will choose their town council chairperson to run their respective towns. Each town council will then notify the Minister of National Development who will declare an area to be a town by order published in the gazette in accordance with Section 3 of the Town Councils Act. The area for a town shall comprise either (a) a single constituency or (b) any two or three constituencies where the MPs agree to their constituencies being declared to be a town. The declaration

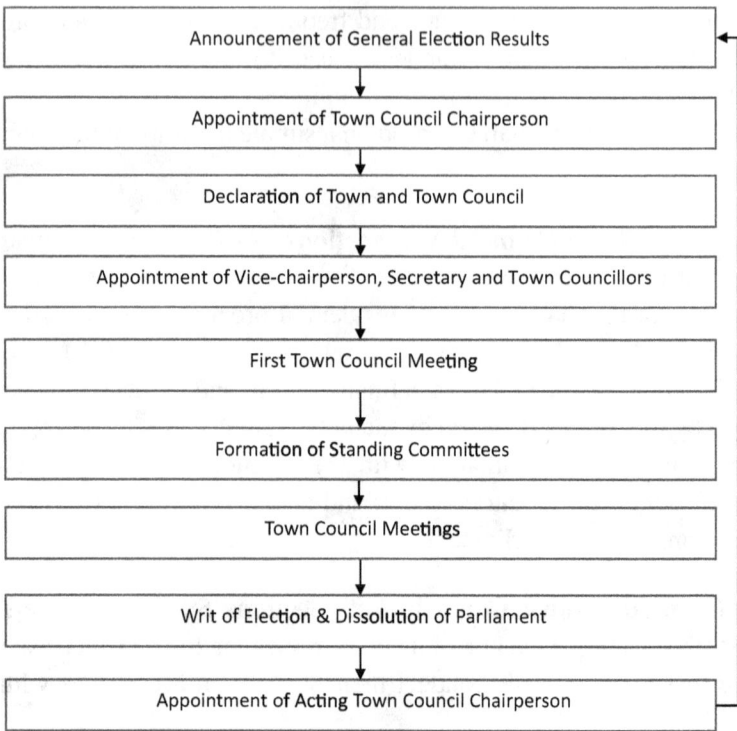

Figure 2.1 Establishment of Town Council

of all towns in the event of a general election following the dissolution of Parliament shall be done on the 14th day after the last date the election results are declared for the respective constituencies and shall be effective from that day.

Within 30 days of assuming office, the town council chairperson shall appoint the vice-chairpersons, secretary and town councillors to form the council. Section 8 of the Town Councils Act states that the chairperson must appoint at least six individuals to be appointed members and the maximum number that may be appointed is the higher of the following:

(a) 10 for each Member of Parliament required to be returned at any parliamentary election for each constituency comprised in the town of that town council or

(b) 30.

To encourage ownership among residents, at least two-thirds of the appointed town councillors must be residents of the HDB estates of the town. The remaining town councillors can be individuals of different expertise to improve the governance of the town councils. Once the council is formed, it will proceed with the setting up of standing committees as follows:

(a) Audit Committee;
(b) Contracts Committee;
(c) Estate Committee;
(d) Finance Committee;
(e) Project Committee; and
(f) Publicity Committee.

Based on its standing order, the town council will commence its meetings and run the town council till the next general election or by-election. Upon the issue of a writ of election and dissolution of Parliament, all elected MPs will cease to be members of the town council. As such, the remaining town councillors will have to elect among themselves an acting town council chairperson to run the council till the appointment of the next elected MP as town council chairperson for the new town council.

The following sections in the Town Councils Act are commonly referred to when running a town council. The key highlights of each section are listed in Table 2.1.

Table 2.1   Key Highlights of the Town Councils Act 1988 of Singapore (revised edition as of 1st December 2021)

(a) Establishment of Town Council		
Section	**Header**	**Description**
3	Declaration of Towns	It empowers the National Development Minister to declare by order published in the Gazette an area to be a Town comprising:
		(a) a single constituency; or
		(b) any 2 or 3 constituencies where the Members of Parliament agree to their constituencies being declared to be a Town.

(*Continued*)

Table 2.1   *(Continued)*

Section	Header	Description
8	Composition of Town Council	It states that a Town Council shall consist of: (a) the elected member or members ex officio; and (b) such other members appointed by the chairperson. The appointed members shall consist of at least 6 individuals and the maximum number to be appointed shall be the higher of the following: (a) 10 for each Member of Parliament in the Town; or (b) 30.
9	Chairperson and vice-chairpersons	The chairperson of the Town Council shall be: (a) the Member of Parliament if the area of the Town comprises only one Single Member Constituency (SMC); or (b) an elected Member of Parliament chosen to be chairperson by the elected members of the Town Council if the area of the Town comprises a single Group Representation Constituency (GRC), or 2 or 3 constituencies.
10 & 11	Duties of chairperson and vice-chairpersons	The chairperson shall preside at meetings of the Town Council and shall perform such duties as prescribed in the Act. He or she shall have an original vote and also, if the votes are equal, a casting vote.
13	Tenure of office of elected members	An elected Member assumes office on the day the town is declared by the Minister. The elected member shall vacate office when he or she ceases to be a Member of Parliament for the constituency comprised within the Town for which the Town Council is established.
14	Tenure of office of appointed members	All appointed members shall hold office for a term of 2 years. The chairperson may, at any time, revoke the appointment of any appointed member without assigning any reason.
15	Conflict of interest and disclosure by members	As soon as practicable after a member of a Town Council becomes aware of a conflict of interest, the member must disclose in writing the fact, nature, character and extent of the personal or financial interest that gives rise to the conflict.

Table 2.1 *(Continued)*

(b) Functions, Powers and Proceedings of Town Council

Section	Header	Description
20	Functions of Town Council	The functions of a Town Council are: (a) to control, manage, maintain and improve the common property of the residential and commercial property in the housing estates of Housing and Development Board (HDB) within the Town for the benefit of the residents of those housing estates and to keep them in a state of good and serviceable repair and in a proper and clean condition; and (b) to exercise such powers and perform such duties as may from time to time be conferred or imposed on the Town Council by or under the Town Councils Act.
21	Powers of Town Council	The Town Council has power to perform the following: (a) To establish and maintain places and facilities on or make improvements to the common property of the residential and commercial property for the benefit of residents of housing estates of the HDB within the Town subject to written consent from HDB. (b) To do, with the approval of the Minister, any of the following in relation to any facility that is erected, installed or planted within the Town but is outside the common property of the residential and commercial property in the HDB estates within the Town: (1) erect, install or plant (including landscaping) the facility, (2) demolish and relocate the facility, and (3) repair and maintain the facility subject to the consent of the owner of the property on which the facility is erected, installed, planted, demolished or relocated. (c) To acquire and hold property of any description if, in the opinion of the Town Council, the property is necessary for the accommodation of the Town Council or for the performance of any purpose

(Continued)

Table 2.1   (*Continued*)

Section	Header	Description
		which the Town Council is required or is permitted by the Town Councils Act to perform and, subject to the terms and conditions upon which the property is held, to dispose of the property.
		(d) To set charges as the Town Council from time to time thinks fit for the use of (1) any common property within the Town or any part of the common property, (2) any improvements made by the Town Council to that common property, and (3) any services and facilities provided by the Town Council.
		(e) To appoint agents to carry out its functions under the Town Councils Act.
		(f) To accept gifts and donations whether of property or otherwise and whether subject to any special trust or not.
		(g) To do all such other acts as are reasonably necessary for the exercise or performance of all or any of the powers or duties of the Town Council under the Town Councils Act and for the enforcement of its by-laws and perform any other function which is incidental or conducive to the attainment or furtherance of the purposes of the Town Council in accordance with the provisions of the Act.
22	Secretary and other staff of Town Council	The Town Council shall appoint an individual, including any appointed member, to be the secretary to the Town Council. The secretary shall be responsible for the proper administration and management of the functions and affairs of the Town Council in accordance with the Act.
23	Duties of Town Council	The duties of the Town Council shall entail the following:
		(a) To control, manage and administer the common property of the residential and commercial property for the benefit of the residents of those estates.

Table 2.1 (*Continued*)

Section	Header	Description
		(b) To properly maintain and keep in a state of good and serviceable repair the common property of the residential and commercial property.
		(c) To contribute such sum towards the premiums to be paid by HDB for the insurance of the common property of the residential and commercial property against damage by fire as the Minister may, by notice in writing to the Town Council, determine.
		(d) To renew or replace any fixtures or fittings comprised in the common property of the residential and commercial property as and when necessary.
		(e) To provide essential maintenance and lift rescue services to the residents of the residential and commercial property.
		(f) To properly maintain and keep in a good and serviceable repair (including landscaping of) the facilities within the Town that is outside the common property of the residential and commercial property in the HDB estates within the Town, where the facilities are erected, installed or planted by the Town Council with the approval of the Minister and the consent of the owner of the property on which the facilities are erected, installed or planted.
		(g) To comply with the provisions of the Act and rules made thereunder.
		(h) To comply with any notice or order served on it by any competent, public or statutory authority requiring the abatement of any nuisance on the common property of the residential and commercial property or ordering repairs or other work to be done in respect of the common property.

(*Continued*)

Table 2.1 (*Continued*)

Section	Header	Description
25	Direction to Town Councils for emergency-related matters	The Minister may, by written direction given to a Town Council (a) require the Town Council to prepare itself to deal with specified kinds of emergency-related purposes or (b) require that (i) access be given to specified kinds of services by the Town Council for specified kinds of emergency-related purposes; or (ii) priority of access be given to specified kinds of services by the Town Council for specified kinds of emergency-related purposes.
26	Power of Town Council to carry out certain works	The Town Council has power to carry out works necessary to rectify any defect which may occur in any pipe, wire, cable, duct or other apparatus within a flat in any residential or commercial property within the Town which is used for or in connection with the carrying, conveying or supplying to such property of water, sewerage, drainage, gas, electricity, garbage or artificially cooled air.
28	By-laws for regulating of housing estates	A Town Council may make by-laws for regulating the control, management and administration, use and enjoyment of the common property of the residential and commercial property in the housing estates within the Town.

(c) Proceedings of Town Council

Section	Header	Description
39	Standing orders	A Town Council may make standing orders to regulate its procedures and meetings.
40	Meetings	A Town Council shall meet at such times as may be laid down in its standing orders and may adjourn from time to time. The notice of meeting shall be given by the secretary to each member of the Town Council at least 2 working days before the day of each meeting, except in the case of an emergency meeting when as long a notice as possible shall be given.
41	Minutes	The minutes of the proceedings of a Town Council shall be kept and authenticated in accordance with its standing orders.

Table 2.1   (*Continued*)

Section	Header	Description
42	Acts of Town Council	All decisions at meetings shall be decided by a majority of the members present and voting. The Town Council or meeting shall have the discretion to decide any matter by circulating papers.
43	Quorum	At any meeting of a Town Council, one-third of the number of members shall constitute a quorum.
45	Committees	A Town Council may, by resolution, appoint such number of committees as it thinks fit for purposes which, in the opinion of the Town Council, would be better regulated and managed by means of such committees.
		At least one-third of the members of each committee formed under this section must be members of the Town Council, and where a committee is formed under this section by a Town Council for any of the following matters:
		(a) Internal audit
		(b) Finance
		(c) Procurement of goods or services
		(d) Publicity and public relations
		(e) Estate management
		The chairperson of each committee must be a member of the Town Council.
46	Delegation of powers	A Town Council may, subject to such conditions or restrictions as it thinks fit, delegate to any member of the Town Council, or to any committee of the Town Council or to any member thereof, all or any of the powers, functions and duties by this Act.
		A Town Council may, subject to such conditions or restrictions as it thinks fit, delegate to any employee thereof or any agent all or any of the powers, functions and duties by this Act.
47	Constitution of Town Council Fund	The Town Council shall establish and maintain separate funds for improvements to and the management and maintenance of residential and commercial property. These funds shall constitute the Town Council Fund.

(*Continued*)

Table 2.1   (*Continued*)

Section	Header	Description
48	Transfer of surpluses after Parliamentary election	After every parliamentary election, the Town Council shall transfer its accumulated operating surpluses in the following manner: (a) if the member or members elected and the previous member or members for the constituency stood in elections for the same political party — 80% of its surpluses relating to such area of the Town comprised in that constituency shall be transferred to the prescribed sinking funds of the Town Council relating to the area; or (b) if the member or members elected and the previous member or members for the constituency stood in elections for different political parties — all its surpluses relating to such area of the Town comprised in that constituency shall be transferred to the prescribed sinking funds of the Town Council relating to the area.
49	Accounts and records	The Town Council has a duty to ensure that the accounts and records are kept in accordance with the Town Councils Financial Rules as follows: (a) Proper accounts and records of the transactions and affairs of the Town Council. (b) Proper and separate accounts for each of the funds established in Section 47(1), 47(4) and 47(5).
50	Annual accounts	The financial year of a Town Council shall begin on 1st April of each year and end on 31st March of the succeeding year. The Town Council shall, within 3 months after the close of each financial year, prepare and submit financial statements in such form as the Auditor-General may direct in respect of that year to the auditor.
51	Estimates	The Town Council shall prepare and display for public inspection in such places within the Town as it may direct, estimates of its revenue and expenditure for the next financial year together with a list of works which the Town Council proposes to undertake during the next financial year not later than one month before the end of the financial year.

Table 2.1 *(Continued)*

Section	Header	Description
52	Audit	The accounts of a Town Council shall be audited by the Auditor-General or such other auditor as may be appointed annually by the Town Council with the approval of the Minister after the Minister has consulted the Auditor-General.
53	Conservancy and service charges	The Town Council may in each month levy conservancy and service charges at such rates as it may determine in accordance with its by-laws in respect of every flat in any residential or commercial property and every stall in any market or food centre of the HDB estates within the Town.
57	Financial rules	The Minister may make financial rules that are consistent with the Town Councils Act for Town Council to carry out its functions and duties.

(d)   Miscellaneous Provisions

Section	Header	Description
66	Recovery of conservancy and service charges from sale of flat	Where any conservancy and service charges levied in respect of any flat by a Town Council remain unpaid on the expiry of the period of 90 days after the Town Council has served on the owner of the flat a written demand for such charges, the charges together with any interest accrued thereon shall constitute a charge on the flat on the expiry of that period in favour of the Town Council. Upon the constitution of the charge on a flat, the Town Council has the power of sale and all other powers relating or incidental thereto to sell and effactually transfer the title to the flat to any purchaser as if the Town Council is a registered mortgagee even though the charge is not registered under the Land Titles Act 1993.
68	Fines to be paid into Town Council Fund	All fines imposed under the Act or any by-law made by a Town Council, less all reasonable legal costs for the prosecution thereof, and all monies collected by it shall be paid into the Town Council Fund.

(Continued)

Table 2.1   (*Continued*)

Section	Header	Description
69	Demand for particulars	A Town Council or any member or employee of a Town Council or any police officer who reasonably believes that any person has committed an offence under the Act or any by-laws or rules made thereunder may require the person to furnish evidence of his or her identity.
70	Liability of owners of vehicles for parking offences	When a parking offence is committed within a Town, the person who, at the time of the commission of the offence, is the owner of the vehicle in respect of which the offence is committed shall be guilty of an offence under any by-law made by the Town Council in all aspects as if he or she were the actual offender guilty of the parking offence unless the court is satisfied that the vehicle was at the relevant time a stolen vehicle or a vehicle illegally taken or used.
71	Personal liability of members, etc., for certain offences	Where a Town Council commits an offence under Section 24(4) or 61(4) of the Act, an individual — (a) who is the chairperson of, or secretary to, the Town Council, or who was purporting to act in any such capacity; and (b) who (i) consented or connived to effect the commission of the offence, (ii) is in any other way, whether by act or omission, knowingly concerned in, or is party to, the commission of the offence by the Town Council, or (iii) knew or ought reasonably to have known that the offence by the Town Council would be or is being committed, and failed to take all reasonable steps to prevent or stop the commission of that offence, shall be guilty of that same offence as is the Town Council, and shall be liable on conviction to a fine not exceeding $5,000 or to imprisonment for a term not exceeding 12 months or to both and, in the case of a continuing offence, to a further fine not exceeding $50 for every day or part of a day during which the offence continues after the conviction.

Table 2.1 (*Continued*)

Section	Header	Description
		Where a Town Council commits an offence under sections 21(8), 25(6), 47(9), or 52(15), Town Councils Financial Rules made under Section 57 or any rule made under Section 82 about the governance of Town Councils, an individual —
		(a) who is the chairperson of, or secretary to, the Town Council, or who was purporting to act in any such capacity; and
		(b) who (i) consented or connived to effect the commission of the offence, (ii) is in any other way, whether by act or omission, knowingly concerned in, or is party to, the commission of the offence by the Town Council, or (iii) knew or ought reasonably to have known that the offence by the Town Council would be or is being committed, and failed to take all reasonable steps to prevent or stop the commission of that offence,
		shall be guilty of that same offence as is the Town Council, and shall be liable on conviction to a fine not exceeding $5,000.
72	Composition of offences	A Town Council may, in its discretion, compound any offence under any by-law made by it and is prescribed in those by-laws as a compoundable offence by collecting from the person reasonably suspected of having committed the offence a sum not exceeding $2,000.
74	Protection from personal liability	No suit or other legal proceedings shall lie personally against any member, officer or employee of a Town Council or other person acting under the direction of a Town Council for anything which is in good faith done or intended to be done in the execution or purported execution of the Act or any other Act.
79	Public servants for purposes of Penal Code	All members, officers and employees of a Town Council and all employees of its managing agent shall be deemed to be public servants for the purposes of the Penal Code 1871.

2.3 Town Councils Financial Rules

Section 57 of the Town Councils Act empowers the Minister to make financial rules for town councils to ensure proper accounting and financial management of the council. This entails the setting up of town council funds, preparation of estimates of revenue and expenditure, management of financial authority, tendering procedures, investments and audits, and submission of financial statements and reports.

The key finance and administration functions of the town council include the following:

- budgeting and control system,
- income and expenditure monitoring,
- arrears management system,
- IT system for financial management,
- issue of Temporary Occupation Licence (TOL) and permit,
- booking of facilities,
- human resource management,
- compliance and submissions,
- town council management report.

To facilitate the key functions of the finance and administration of the town council, a yearly checklist of tasks is compiled, as listed in Table 2.2. The financial year of a town council starts from 1st April to 31st March of the following year.

Table 2.2 Checklist for Finance and Administration Management

Month	Tasks
April	• File income tax returns (by Inland Revenue Authority of Singapore's submission due date).
	• Quarterly transfer of sinking fund and Lift Replacement Fund (LRF) and submission of LRF matching grant (by 30 April).
	• Quarterly GST subvention claims (by 30 April).
	• File GST returns.
	• Submit Chairperson's declaration for Managing Agent's participation of Town Council's tender to the Ministry of National Development (MND).

Table 2.2   (*Continued*)

Month	Tasks
	• Month-end closing of accounts. • Monthly returns to MND and TC secretariat (Arrears report for TCMR). • Prepare for year-end closing.
May	• Month-end closing of accounts. • Monthly returns to MND and TC secretariat (Arrears report for TCMR). • Prepare for year-end closing.
June	• Annual estimates (to publish budget in gazette on or before 30 June). • Submit draft accounts to MND (by 30 June). • Month-end closing of accounts. • Monthly returns to MND and TC secretariat (Arrears report for TCMR).
July	• Quarterly transfer of sinking fund and LRF and submission of LRF matching grant (by 31 July). • Quarterly GST subvention claims (by 31 July). • File GST returns. • Submit Chairperson's declaration for Managing Agent's participation of Town Council's tender to the MND. • Month-end closing of accounts. • Monthly returns to MND and TC secretariat (Arrears report for TCMR).
August	• Finalise external audit and submit annual report to MND. • Month-end closing of accounts. • Monthly returns to MND and TC secretariat (Arrears report for TCMR).
September	• Month-end closing of accounts. • Monthly returns to MND and TC secretariat (Arrears report for TCMR).
October	• Quarterly transfer of sinking fund and LRF and submission of LRF matching grant (by 31 October). • Quarterly GST subvention claims (by 31 October). • File GST returns. • Submit Chairperson's declaration for Managing Agent's participation of Town Council's tender to the Ministry of National Development (MND). • Month-end closing of accounts. • Monthly returns to MND and TC secretariat (Arrears report for TCMR).
November	• Month-end closing of accounts. • Monthly returns to MND and TC secretariat (Arrears report for TCMR).
December	• Month-end closing of accounts. • Monthly returns to MND and TC secretariat (Arrears report for TCMR).

(*Continued*)

Table 2.2   *(Continued)*

Month	Tasks
January	• File property tax (by 31 January). • Quarterly transfer of sinking fund, and LRF and submission of LRF matching grant (by 31 January). • Quarterly GST subvention claims (by 31 January). • File GST returns. • Submit Chairperson's declaration for Managing Agent's participation of Town Council's tender to the Ministry of National Development (MND). • Month-end closing of accounts. • Monthly returns to MND and TC secretariat (Arrears report for TCMR).
February	• Annual estimates (town council's budget to be approved by Town Council on or before 28 February) in accordance with Town Councils Act. • Display of annual estimates for public inspection (notice board and website) in accordance with Town Councils Act. • Month-end closing of accounts. • Monthly returns to MND and TC secretariat (Arrears report for TCMR).
March	• Appointment of auditors. • Month-end closing of accounts. • Monthly returns to MND and TC secretariat (Arrears report for TCMR).

2.4 Town Council By-laws

A town council may make by-laws for regulating the control, management, administration, use and enjoyment of the common property of the residential and commercial property in the HDB estates within the town and generally for the purposes of exercising its powers and carrying out its duties and functions under the Town Councils Act. The by-laws will usually cover the following areas:

(a) prescribing the administrative fee to be paid by any person in respect of any services provided by the town council or any debt due to the town council;

(b) prohibiting or regulating the parking of vehicles on common property other than parking places;

(c) prescribing the penalty to be paid by the town council's licensees or by any owner or tenant of any flat leased from the HDB for late payment of any conservancy and service charges or licence fee due to the town council;

(d) requiring deposits to be placed with the town council by any owner or tenant of any flat leased from the HDB to secure the payment of conservancy and service charges; and

(e) prescribing the offences which may be compounded.

Table 2.3 lists out the common by-laws made by the town council in managing its estates.

Table 2.3   Common By-laws of Town Council

S/no	By-Laws	Description
1	Dumping and renovation debris	(a) No person shall place, deposit or leave, or cause or permit to be placed, deposited, kept or left, any material, article, object or thing on any common property or in any open space except in such common property or open space designated by the Town Council for that purpose.
		(b) No person shall transport any renovation debris or other building material in any lift in a building in any housing estate, or over any other common property, except with the prior written permission of the Town Council.
		(c) No person shall place, deposit, keep or leave or cause or permit to be placed, deposited, kept or left any trade refuse on any common property or in any open space except in a refuse or litter container or receptacle designated for that purpose.
2	Obstruction of common property	(a) No person shall obstruct or cause or permit the obstruction of the lawful use of any common property with any object, fixture or thing.
		(b) The Town Council may remove and detain any object, fixture or thing obstructing the lawful use of any common property.
		(c) The Town Council shall immediately give written notice to the owner or person having lawful possession of the object, fixture, or thing removed and detained by the Town Council that he or she may, on payment of the expenses incurred by

(Continued)

Table 2.3 (*Continued*)

S/no	By-Laws	Description
		the Town Council in such removal and detention, claim possession from the Town Council within 30 days of such removal and detention.
		(d) If the object, fixture or thing removed and detained by the Town Council is not claimed by the owner or person having lawful possession thereof within 30 days of such removal and detention, the Town Council may (i) dispose of it by public auction or otherwise, and (ii) apply the proceeds of the sale to the expenses incurred by the Town Council in the removal and detention, and the surplus, if any, shall be paid to such owner or person having lawful possession thereof.
3	Damage to common property	(a) No person shall remove, destroy, damage or deface, or remove any earth or soil from, any common property.
		(b) No person shall remove, destroy, damage or vandalise any facility on any common property or in an open space.
		(c) The costs and expenses, including administrative costs incurred by the Town Council in restoring any damaged common property or facility to its conditions before such removal, destruction, damage, defacement or vandalism or in replacing earth or soil or any other property that has been removed shall constitute a debt due to the Town Council and shall be recoverable as such.
4	Misuse of common property and open spaces	No person shall bathe, wash, wade, swim, fish or cause or permit any animal belonging to him or her or under his or her charge to enter, or to remove any thing from any pond, lake or fountain maintained by the Town Council.
5	Damage to turf, plant, shrub or tree	(a) No person shall remove, cut, damage or dispose of any turf, plant, shrub or tree or part thereof situated on any common property or in any open space.
		(b) No person shall pick a shrub or plant or any part thereof situated on any common property or in any open space.
		(c) No person shall plant, cultivate or grow, or cause or permit to be planted, cultivated or grown, any plant, shrub or tree on any common property or in an open space without prior written permission of the Town Council.
		(d) No person shall cause or permit any plant, shrub or tree belonging to him or her to damage or encroach into any common property or open space.

Table 2.3 (*Continued*)

S/no	By-Laws	Description
6	Unlawful parking	(a) No person shall park any vehicle on common property or in an open space except in a parking place.
		(b) No person shall use, ride or drive on any common property or in any open space any vehicle other than a perambulator, a child's toy vehicle used solely be a child or wheel-chair used solely for the conveyance of persons suffering from some physical defect or disability.
7	Power to detain or remove vehicles	(1) Where a vehicle is parked on any common property or in any open space in contravention of any by-law, or it appears to the secretary or officer authorised by the Town Council that any vehicle which has broken down or been permitted to remain at rest on any common property or in any open space, has been abandoned without lawful authority, the secretary or officer authorised by the Town Council —
		(a) may detain the vehicle by any means, including preventing the removal of the vehicle without the consent of the secretary or authorised officer by fixing an immobilisation device to the vehicle, and if the vehicle is detained, shall give notice in writing of the detention to the owner or person who had lawful possession of the vehicle when it was detained that he or she may, on payment of the expenses incurred by the Town Council in respect of such detention, claim possession of the vehicle within 7 days of such notice being served on him or her; and
		(b) if such owner or person cannot be located upon reasonable inquiry being made by the Town Council, may cause to be displayed such notice at the nearest block's notice board,
		(2) Where any vehicle is removed under this rule in the by-law to a place of safety, the secretary shall, within all reasonable dispatch, give notice in writing of the removal to the owner or person who had lawful possession of the vehicle when it was removed that he or she may, on payment of the expenses incurred by the Town Council in respect of such removal, claim possession of the vehicle within 30 days of such removal.

(*Continued*)

2.5 Town Council Code of Governance

The Ministry of National Development has developed a code of governance for town councils in 2019. The main purpose of the code is to promote greater transparency and raise the standard of corporate governance of town councils. The code was effective from 1 April 2020 and has provided a framework for town councils to adopt best practices to fulfil their fiduciary duties and improve public accountability.

The objectives of the code are as follows:

(a) Enhance the effectiveness of town councils by sharing recommended governance practices.
(b) Provide guidance to the town councilors to guide them to carry out their fiduciary duties.
(c) Improve the transparency of town councils' operations to build public trust and confidence.

The Code is based on five guiding principles as follows:

(a) **Integrity**: The town council acts with integrity in its decision-making and execution of its duties and in the best interests of the residents.
(b) **Objectivity**: The town council exercises objective judgement that represents the interests of the residents.
(c) **Accountability**: The town council is accountable to the residents for the way it exercises its mandated duties. The town council fulfils its responsibilities to enable the effective running of the town council in the best interests of the residents.
(d) **Fairness**: The town council is fair and impartial in its interactions with the residents.
(e) **Transparency**: The town council maintains open communication with the residents in the conduct and execution of its duties.

The code is applicable in four key aspects of township management: (i) council effectiveness, (ii) internal controls and processes, (iii) financial management and (iv) vendor management. To facilitate compliance of the code, the Ministry has provided a corporate governance disclosure checklist as shown in Table 2.4 for town councils to declare their compliance

Table 2.4   Corporate Governance Disclosure Checklist

(a)   Council Effectiveness

Town council plan

---

1   The council ensures that the town council plan:

    (a) outlines the long-term goals of the town council;

    (b) is aligned with the future plans of the town council;

    (c) is understood by the town council, management, town council staff and residents;

    (d) aligns all expenditure and investments with its defined goals and objectives; and

    (e) is reviewed and updated periodically.

2   The council conducts regular self-evaluation to assess its performance and effectiveness in achieving the town council's objectives and plan.

Town councillors

---

3   The attendance of each town councillor at council meetings is recorded, circulated to the council for information, and reported to the council chairperson at least on an annual basis.

Composition and structure

---

4   There are written terms of reference for the council and each of its council committees, which clearly set out the authority and duties.

5   The chairperson of the committee overseeing audit matters does not chair or is not a member in other council committees.

6   The majority of the members of the committee overseeing audit matters are not concurrently members in the other council committees.

7   The chairperson of the committee overseeing finance matters does not chair or is not a member in other council committees that oversee procurement matters.

8   The majority of the members of the committee overseeing finance are not concurrently members in the other council committees that oversee procurement matters.

9   The town council has processes in place for the selection and appointment of town councillors and discloses a description of the process in the town council's annual report.

10   Roles and responsibilities of designated positions in the council are clearly defined and documented.

11   There is a maximum limit of 10 consecutive years for a chairperson of any council committee that oversees these areas:

    (a) audit and risk management;

    (b) finance; and

    (c) procurement of goods and services.

(Continued)

Table 2.4   (*Continued*)

12	Induction which includes an orientation programme is provided to all incoming town councillors.

(b)   Internal Controls and Processes

Risk management and internal controls

13	The council discloses in the annual report whether it has carried out an assessment of key risks facing the town council and whether internal controls in place are adequate and effective.
14	The council has established a business continuity plan and regularly conducts appropriate and complete tests to evaluate the functionality and effectiveness of the plan.
15	There are documented communication policies in place regarding the release of information about the town council and its activities.

Internal audit

16	The council has established an effective internal audit function that reports directly to the committee overseeing internal audit.
17	The internal audit function is independent of the activities it audits.
18	The committee that oversees internal audit reviews the adequacy and effectiveness of the internal audit function at least annually.

Record keeping

19	The town council retains ownership of all town council related documents and ensures all records are properly maintained and kept up-to-date.

Data privacy and protection

20	The town council has a data governance and information security framework with adequate and effective internal controls embedded in the policies and procedures.
21	Town councillors, committee members, town council staff, employees of managing agents and other parties are aware of the requirements for adequate data privacy and protection of confidential and sensitive data if they have sight of confidential and sensitive data.
22	Town councillors, committee members, town council staff, employees of managing agents and other parties undergo training on data privacy and protection requirements if they are involved in the handling of confidential and sensitive data to fulfil their duties.

Table 2.4 *(Continued)*

23	There is a proper response plan in place to promptly detect, report, resolve and recover from any unauthorised access, modification, use, disclosure, disposal, or activities of similar risk, relating to data in the possession or control of the Town Council.

Human resources

24	There are approved documented human resource policies for Town Council staff, including areas such as:

- recruitment;
- renumeration;
- benefits;
- training and development;
- performance appraisal;
- disciplinary actions; and
- cessation of employment.

25	There is a documented Code of Conduct in place for Town Councillors, Committee Members, Town Council staff and other parties acting on behalf of the Town Council.
26	There is a performance evaluation system in place that regularly monitors and appraises the performance of the Town Council staff. This performance evaluation process is equitable and transparent.
27	There is a process to identify the training needs of all Town Council staff so as to equip them with the necessary skills to adequately perform their role.
28	Staff who are related to Town Councillors or Town Council staff declare such relationships and ensure that they are not involved in any decision making relating to the recruitment, performance evaluation and renumeration of that staff.

Whistleblowing

29	The Town Council has established a whistleblowing policy and its procedures, and discloses the existence of the policy and procedures.

(c) Financial Management

Budgeting and planning

30	The Town Council has a documented process in place to regularly plan and review its current and long-term finances, with the purpose of ensuring proper and efficient management of funds.

(Continued)

Table 2.4 (*Continued*)

31	The Council is regularly briefed at council meetings on the current and projected financial position of the Town Council. Financial statements with comparable budget figures together with analysis and explanations of any variances, are presented at the council meetings.

Reporting on financial information

32	The Council reviews and addresses significant financial reporting issues brought up by the auditors to ensure the integrity and accuracy of the financial statements of the Town Council.

Investment of funds

33	Town Council investments are performed in accordance with the approved investment policy.
34	Returns of all invested funds are regularly reviewed and presented at the council meetings.

(d)   Vendor Management

Procurement

35	The Council ensures the confidentiality of all procurement activities so that no interested bidder, including incumbent vendors and the Managing Agent, is conferred an unfair advantage for the tender.
36	The invitations to tender, names of participating tenderers and their offers, and the name and tender price of the successful tenderer are posted on publicly available channels.

Performance management

37	There is a formal performance evaluation process for the Managing Agent and vendors. Their performance is based on pre-defined criteria by the Council.

annually. If town councils opt not to comply with the code, they will be required to provide meaningful explanations on how the governance standards in the code can be achieved.

(i) **Council effectiveness**: The town council must lay out a town council plan in a formal and structured manner so as to keep its residents and stakeholders informed. The plan shall consist of short-term (3–5 years) and long-term plans (beyond 5 years). These plans will enable the town councils to better allocate their resources and monitor the effectiveness of its implementation of routine maintenance, cyclical maintenance and estate upgrading works. In addition, the town council must communicate the plan to its council, staff, residents and stakeholders so as to encourage active participation when implementing the plan. Very often, town councils will provide a 5- or 10-year master plan which will outline the key maintenance programmes and improvement projects for the next 5 or 10 years in the town. The council may adopt different approaches to gather feedback and ideas from its residents and stakeholders, such as through its feedback channels, town hall meetings or exhibitions. At the same time, the town council will also provide an annual report on its achievements and submit it to Parliament for public scrutiny. The town council chairperson must provide leadership and guidance to ensure that the town council executes its duties effectively and efficiently in accordance with the Town Councils Act and relevant legislations. The chairperson shall appoint the right mix of town councillors with the relevant skills and expertise to facilitate decision-making. There must be processes in place for the selection, appointment and induction of town councillors. The terms of reference for councillors and town council standing committees must be clearly defined. The key responsibilities of the chairperson are as follows:

- Lead and chair the council to fulfil its duties and responsibilities to serve the needs of residents and stakeholders.
- Plan and execute both short-term and long-term plans (master plan) of the council to fulfill the aspirations of residents and stakeholders.
- Ensure compliance with Town Councils Act and the relevant legislations, including promoting good corporate governance.
- Provide relevant information to allow objective decision-making by the council and effective communication with residents and stakeholders.
- Promote a culture of integrity, honesty and openness in the council.
- Encourage active engagement and participation of residents and stakeholders.
- Develop unique characteristics and identity for the town to promote a sense of belonging and ownership.

(ii) **Internal controls and processes**: The town council must set up an effective risk management and internal controls system to manage the potential risks of its operations. These include documented policies, checks and balances measures, standard operating procedures and business continuity plans to reduce disruptions to the town council services during a crisis. The council should have documented policies and procedures in place for managing conflicts of interest. It should have an independent audit function that will provide an independent and objective assessment of the effectiveness of its internal controls system. As the town council handles personal and sensitive information of its residents and stakeholders, it must have a robust data privacy and information security system to safeguard the confidentiality, integrity and availability of the information, especially against cyberattacks. The council should also have a code of conduct and professional ethics to guide its councillors, staff and service providers. A whistle-blowing policy must be established to allow individuals to raise issues of concern in confidence to the town council.

(iii) **Financial management**: The town council must develop a sound financial management system to manage its assets and funds in accordance with the Town Councils Act and Town Councils Financial Rules. The council should have financial plans for the allocation of funds to carry out short-term and long-term maintenance works for the benefit of its residents. Financial information should be provided to the council on a regular and timely basis so as to facilitate informed decision-making by the council. The council should adopt an investment policy to invest its surplus funds in accordance with the directives from the ministry and Town Councils Act.

(iv) **Vendor management**: The town council must set up processes to manage its procurement processes and monitor the performance of its vendors to achieve the desired level of service standards. There must be policies and procedures in place to ensure that contracts are awarded to suitable vendors, that can provide the best value proposition. The council should have a performance evaluation system to ensure that vendors provide quality services to meet the needs and requirements of the residents and stakeholders.

Chapter 3

Town Council Setup, Organisation and Structure

3.1 Setting up a Town Council

As town councils are political in nature, it is crucial for elected Members of Parliament (MPs) to follow the Town Councils Act closely when establishing a town and appointing the town councillors. To ensure transparency and accountability to the residents of the respective towns, the declaration of a town and appointment of town councillors are required to be published in the government gazette for public scrutiny. The key processes in the setting up of a town council are shown in Figure 2.1.

After every general election or by-election, the elected MP or MPs will decide an area which may comprise a single constituency or any two or three constituencies to be declared as a town. Section 3(1) of the Town Councils Act states as follows: "For the purposes of constituting a Town Council to control, manage, maintain and improve the common property of residential and commercial property in the housing and development estates of the Board in any area, the Minister may, from time to time, by order published in the Gazette, declare to be a Town by such name as the Minister may designate in the order an area comprising:- (a) a single con-stituency; (b) any 2 or 3 constituencies where the MPs agree to their constituencies being declared to be a Town." For example, the elected MP for Bukit Panjang Single Member Constituency may declare Bukit Panjang HDB estates as a town to be managed by Bukit Panjang Town Council, or the elected MPs for Holland-Bukit Timah Group Representation

Constituency and Bukit Panjang Single Member Constituency may come together and declare their respective HDB estates to form Holland-Bukit Panjang Town to be managed by Holland-Bukit Panjang Town Council.

Upon the declaration of a Town, the elected MP or MPs will assume office as chairperson, vice-chairpersons and elected members of the town council. Section 9(1) of the Town Councils Act states that: "Subject to subsection (3), a chairperson of a Town Council for a Town is:

a)   If the area of the Town comprises only one single Member constituency, the Member of Parliament for that constituency; and
b)   If the area of the Town comprises a single group representation constituency, or 2 or 3 constituencies, whoever is chosen by the elected members of the Town Council from among themselves to be the chairperson."

Once the Town Council chairperson assumes office, he or she shall proceed to appoint Town Councillors to form the town council in accordance with Section 8 of the Town Councils Act. The composition of the town council is as follows:

Section 8(1) states that: "A Town Council shall consist of:-

a)   the elected member or members ex officio; and
b)   such other members appointed by the chairperson in accordance with subsections (2) and (3)."

Section 8(2) states that: "The chairperson shall, within 30 days of assuming his or her office, appoint the members under subsection (1)(b) on the nomination of the elected members, each of whom (including the chairperson) may nominate such number of members as they may agree or if they fail to agree, an equal number of members, of whom not less than two-thirds shall be residents of any housing estate of the Board within the Town."

Section 8(3) states that: "At least 6 individuals must be appointed under subsection (1)(b) as appointed members of a Town Council, but the maximum number that may be so appointed is the higher of the following:-

a) 10 for each Member of Parliament required to be returned at any parliamentary election for each constituency comprised in the Town of that Town Council;

b) 30."

Thus, the composition of the Town Council shall consist of both elected town councillors (elected MPs) and appointed town councillors (volunteers). In order to allow participation by residents in the decision-making, at least two-third of the appointed town councillors must be residents of the housing estates within the town. As volunteers, appointed town councillors may be paid allowances out of the town council funds.

Section 13 of the Town Councils Act states that: "A Member of Parliament assumes office as an elected member of a town council-

a) for a town declared after a general election — on the day that the order made under section 3(1) in the circumstances in section 3(3) takes effect;

b) for a town comprising any constituency in which a by-election is held, on the day after the day he or she is declared returned at the by-election as the Member of Parliament for that constituency under Section 49(7E)(a) or 49A(5) of the Parliamentary Elections Act 1954, whichever happens; or

c) for a town in any other case — on the day the town is declared under section 3."

The tenure of office for appointed town councillors shall be 2 years and they shall be eligible for reappointment. An elected town councillor shall vacate his or her office as an elected member of a town council when he or she ceases to be an MP for the constituency comprised within the town for which the town council is established. Upon the appointment of town councillors, the chairperson shall set up the various standing committees for the council, such as audit committee, contracts committee, estate committee, finance committee, project committee and publicity committee. The council will then hold a meeting to appoint the town council secretary and decide on the mode of management for the town.

There are three common modes of management adopted by town councils:

(1) **Managing Agent Approach**: The town council can decide to outsource the management of the town to a managing agent firm which will provide the staff and professional services to manage the town.
(2) **Direct Management Approach**: The town council can decide to manage the town itself by employing its own team of staff.
(3) **Hybrid Approach**: The town council can decide to employ key management staff (General Manager and Property Managers) directly while outsourcing the remaining staff to a managing agent firm.

The most common approach adopted by many town councils is the appointment of a managing agent firm which provides a range of services to manage the town on behalf of the council. To ensure good corporate governance, the town council must exercise due diligence in appointing the managing agent in accordance with the Town Councils Act. The key processes involved in the appointment of a managing agent are shown in Figure 3.1. The scope of work for the managing agent will include the following:

(i) **Preparatory works for taking over town council**
   - Take over town council management.
   - Take over all assets, inventories and keys.
   - Take over all operations, maintenance manuals and as-built drawings.
   - Inform all relevant parties of change in office bearers and town council information.
   - Prepare new organisation chart and inspect estates.
(ii) **Maintenance management services**
   - Take over common property for new and upgraded estates.
   - Plan maintenance programs (routine and cyclical maintenance works).
   - Tender and contract administration for maintenance and upgrading works.
   - Supervise contractors for maintenance works.

- Proper upkeep of documents, records and as-built drawings.
- Compliance of notices and licences by authorities.
- Lift testing and negotiation for servicing agreement.
- Prepare monthly maintenance report for town council meetings.

(iii) **Accounting and financial services**
- Charge and collect service and conservancy charges and other charges payable to the town council.
- Recover any such sums of money falling due which comprises the preparation of demand letters, and submission of filings to the Small Claims Tribunal.
- Keep proper records and accounts in accordance with the Town Councils Act, Town Councils Financial Rules and relevant legislations.
- Prepare annual and supplementary budgets.
- Prepare monthly management reports and accounts for town council meetings.
- Prepare annual accounts in accordance with statutory requirements.
- Liaise with the Auditor-General or such other auditors as may be appointed annually on the audit of the annual accounts.
- Maintain and manage the funds of the Town Council.

(iv) **Administrative and secretarial services**
- Attend to all correspondences relating to the common property on behalf of the town council.
- Deal with complaints, queries and feedback relating to the common property and take follow-up action accordingly.
- Advise on and arrange for insurance policies against fire, public liability, work injury compensation, all risks and other insurances for the town council.
- Maintain proper records pertaining to town council matters.
- Manage the register of owners and tenants.
- Provide secretarial services at town council, standing committees and *ad-hoc* meetings.

(v) **Corporate communication services**
- Manage town council public relations and communication matters, including media relations.

- Work out an overall communication strategy and response plan to manage public outcry and complaints from various channels, including social media.
- Provide editorial support for the publishing of the town council newsletter and annual reports, including the calling of tender for printing services.
- Improve the image and identity of the town.

(vi) **Optional services**

- Provide project and consultancy services for upgrading projects or special projects.
- Provide professional engineers' services (Licensed Electrical Worker) for the application of or renewal of licences for electrical installations.
- Provide customer satisfaction surveys to evaluate the quality of services provided by the town council.
- Provide carpark management and hawker centre management services.
- Provide any other services as requested by the town council that is within the scope of township management.

3.2 Organisation and Structure of Town Council

Figure 3.2 shows the organisational chart of a typical town council in which the town council chairperson oversees the various standing committees. The chairperson is assisted by one or two vice-chairpersons and the secretary.

Figure 3.3 shows the organisational chart of a typical town council management team comprising a general manager, property managers, property officers, finance and administrative staff, and public relations officers.

3.3 Terms of Reference for Standing Committees

The terms of reference for the various standing committees are as follows:

```
┌─────────────────────────────────────────────────────────────────────┐
│           Town Council decides to appoint Managing Agent (MA)         │
└─────────────────────────────────────────────────────────────────────┘
                                    │
                                    ▼
┌─────────────────────────────────────────────────────────────────────┐
│   Town Council to appoint a project consultant to prepare tender for MA appointment │
└─────────────────────────────────────────────────────────────────────┘
                                    │
                                    ▼
┌─────────────────────────────────────────────────────────────────────┐
│            Project consultant will prepare tender specifications      │
└─────────────────────────────────────────────────────────────────────┘
                                    │
                                    ▼
┌─────────────────────────────────────────────────────────────────────┐
│     Tender specifications will be approved by Tender & Contracts Committee │
└─────────────────────────────────────────────────────────────────────┘
                                    │
                                    ▼
┌─────────────────────────────────────────────────────────────────────┐
│           Town Council will call for open tender for MA appointment   │
└─────────────────────────────────────────────────────────────────────┘
                                    │
                                    ▼
┌─────────────────────────────────────────────────────────────────────┐
│            Project consultant will prepare tender evaluation report   │
└─────────────────────────────────────────────────────────────────────┘
                                    │
                                    ▼
┌─────────────────────────────────────────────────────────────────────┐
│  Tender & Contracts Committee will recommend the award of MA contract to Town Council │
└─────────────────────────────────────────────────────────────────────┘
                                    │
                                    ▼
┌─────────────────────────────────────────────────────────────────────┐
│              Town Council will approve the award of MA contract       │
└─────────────────────────────────────────────────────────────────────┘
                                    │
                                    ▼
┌─────────────────────────────────────────────────────────────────────┐
│                      Town Council will appoint MA                     │
└─────────────────────────────────────────────────────────────────────┘
```

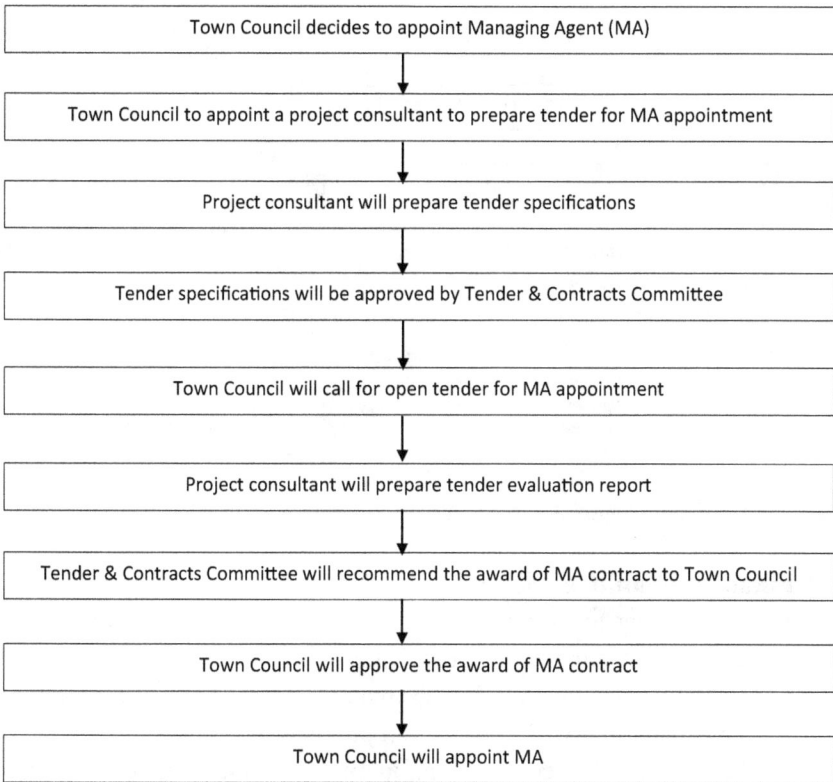

Figure 3.1   Appointment of Managing Agent

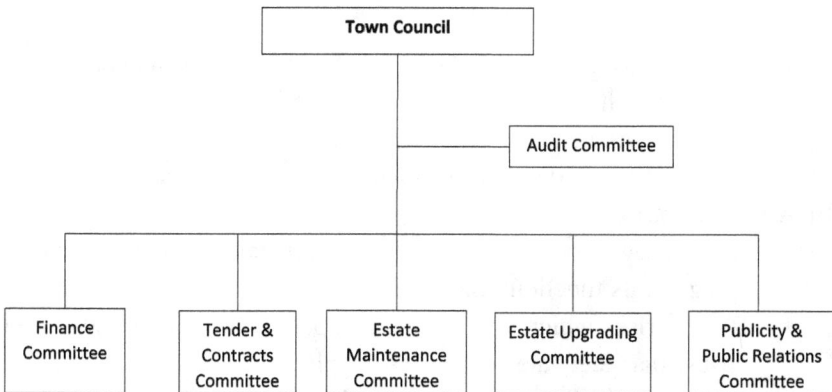

```
                        ┌──────────────────┐
                        │   Town Council   │
                        └──────────────────┘
                                 │
                                 │         ┌──────────────────┐
                                 ├─────────│  Audit Committee │
                                 │         └──────────────────┘
    ┌──────────┬──────────┬──────┴──────┬──────────┬──────────┐
┌─────────┐┌─────────┐┌─────────┐┌────────────┐┌─────────────┐
│ Finance ││Tender & ││ Estate  ││   Estate   ││ Publicity & │
│Committee││Contracts││Maintenance││ Upgrading ││Public Relations│
│         ││Committee││Committee ││ Committee  ││  Committee  │
└─────────┘└─────────┘└─────────┘└────────────┘└─────────────┘
```

Figure 3.2   Organisation Structure of a Town Council

```
                        ┌─────────────────┐
                        │   Chairperson   │
                        └─────────────────┘

                        ┌─────────────────┐
                        │ General Manager │
                        └─────────────────┘
```

Property Managers	Finance Managers	Public Relations Managers	Lift Maintenance Unit
Property Officers	Finance & Administration Executives	Public Relations Executives	
Horticulture Officers	Customer Relations Assistants	Public Relations Assistants	IT Support Unit
			Call Centre

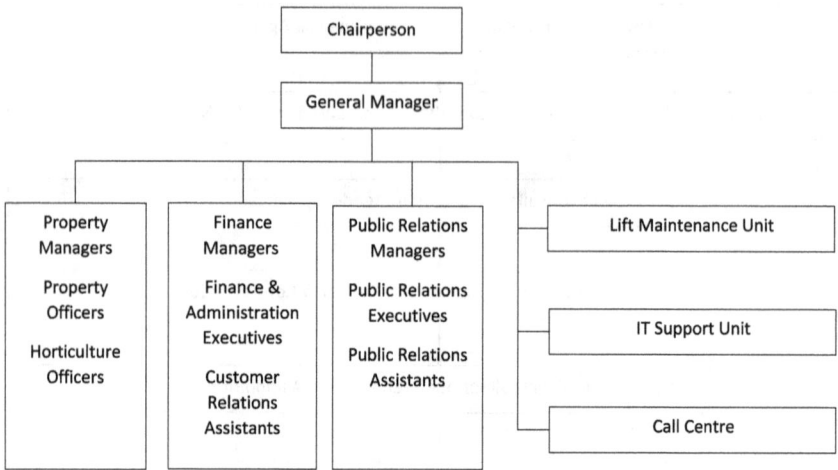

Figure 3.3 Town Council Management Team

(a) **Finance committee**
  • Ensure that town council complies with the Town Councils Act and Town Councils Financial Rules.
  • Provide oversight on all finance matters relating to the town council.
  • Formulate financial policies and procedures.
  • Ensure internal controls are in place to attain good corporate governance.
  • Be involved in the budget preparation process.
  • Review and monitor town council's financial performance regularly.
  • Monitor town council's service and conservancy charges arrears and establish arrears management guidelines.
  • Make recommendations for the investment of surplus funds and monitor the returns on investment.

(b) **Audit committee**
  • Review town council's reporting structure and procedures for carrying out its functions and duties.
  • Review risks which town council's operations are exposed to and ensure that adequate controls are in place.
  • Review the findings from the annual audits, recommend follow-up actions and evaluate their effectiveness.

- Review financial reporting issues highlighted by the internal or external auditors in consultation with the finance committee.
- Ensure the availability of feedback channels for town councillors and staff to report improprieties in the town council (whistle-blowing policy).

(c) **Tender and contracts committee**

- Review town council's procurement Standard Operating Procedures (SOPs) and tender specifications regularly to ensure that its contents remain relevant.
- Ensure that the Town Council's procurement processes comply with Town Councils Act and Town Councils Financial rules.
- Ensure that procurement contracts are carried in a fair and transparent manner and provide good value for money.
- Evaluate and recommend the award of contracts.
- Ensure proper documentation of tender and evaluation processes.
- Ensure that the town council has an effective system to monitor the performance of contractors.

(d) **Estate maintenance committee**

- Ensure a clean and safe environment.
- Ensure that the town council has an effective system to monitor the performance of contractors and respond promptly to feedback from residents and tenants.
- Plan long term for cyclical maintenance works.
- Formulate, implement and review by-laws or policies governing the management of common property.
- Monitor the essential maintenance services for the breakdown of services such as water supply, electrical failure, lift rescue operations, and building systems.
- Monitor the enforcement actions taken in the estates, such as illegal outdoor display areas, illegal parking on common areas or unauthorised installations.
- Explore and recommend new technologies for better estate maintenance.

(e) **Estate upgrading committee**

- Spearhead the development of a master plan (5–10 years plan) for the town.

- Review the provision of functional and recreation facilities within the town.
- Gather feedback from residents and stakeholders for town improvement works.
- Provide support in gathering consensus for upgrading programmes, such as the Neighbourhood Renewal Programme.
- Provide inputs to the tender and contracts committee to facilitate the calling of tenders for improvement works.
- Monitoring and reviewing the progress of improvement works.
- Establish procedures for staff to manage feedback and complaints from residents and tenants arising from the improvement works.

(f) **Publicity and public relations committee**
- Enhance the image of the town council.
- Establish customer service delivery SOPs to improve town council services.
- Improve communication between town council and its residents/tenants to enhance the community spirit.
- Organise education campaigns or programmes with residents and stakeholders to promote gracious, harmonious and quality living.
- Publicise town council's activities through newsletters and other publicity materials.
- Manage media relations including social media.
- Promote good relations among residents and stakeholders.

3.4 Town Council Meetings

Section 40 of the Town Councils Act states that: "A town council must meet at such times as may be laid down in its standing orders and may adjourn from time to time." Town councils will normally hold council meetings bi-monthly while the standing committees will meet in between the council meetings. The secretary of the council must give adequate notice of meeting based on the provisions in the Town Councils Act and the town council's standing order. The minutes of the proceedings of the town council and its committee must be kept and authenticated in accordance with the standing orders. At any meeting of the town council, one-third of the number of members shall constitute a quorum. The quorum for any committee must be laid down in the standing orders of the town council. The chairperson of the town council and various standing committees shall preside over the town council meetings and standing committee meetings, respectively.

3.5 Budgeting and Reports

Section 51 of the Town Councils Act states that "not later than one month before the end of each financial year, a town council must prepare, and display for public inspection in such places within the town as it may direct, estimates of its revenue and expenditure for the next financial year together with a list of works which the town council proposes to undertake during the next financial year". The estimates must set out the sources of revenue and the distribution of expenditure under separate headings. The list of proposed works must include the types of projects, cost estimates and project duration.

The town council will usually start budget preparations in the month of October of each financial year. The finance standing committee shall oversee the preparation of the estimates and submit this to the council for approval. The key steps in budget preparation are shown in Figure 3.4. A sample of the income and expenditure budget statement for a financial year is shown in Table 3.1.

The income estimates will entail the following tasks:

(a) Determining the dwelling units for various flat types and other properties for the next financial year based on projections of the number of dwelling units to be taken over or demolished for the next financial year.

(b) Determining the number of car and motorcycle parking lots for the next financial year based on projections of the number of properties to be taken over or demolished for the next financial year.

(c) Determining the Service and Conservancy Charges (S&CC) income for the next financial year based on projections of the existing or proposed revised S&CC rates for the next financial year.

General manager will initiate the annual budget preparations for next financial year

↓

Finance manager and property managers will prepare the income and expenditure estimates

↓

Finance manager will collate and draft the proposed budget

↓

General manager will approve the draft budget

↓

Draft budget will be presented to the Finance Standing Committee for approval

↓

Finance Standing Committee will approve and submit the draft budget to Town Council for approval

↓

Town Council will approve the budget for the next financial year by 28 February and publish the approved budget in the government gazette by 30 June

↓

Town Council will display the approved budget on the noticeboard and website by the last day of February

↓

Town Council will revise the budget if necessary during the financial year and publish the approved supplementary budget in the government gazette

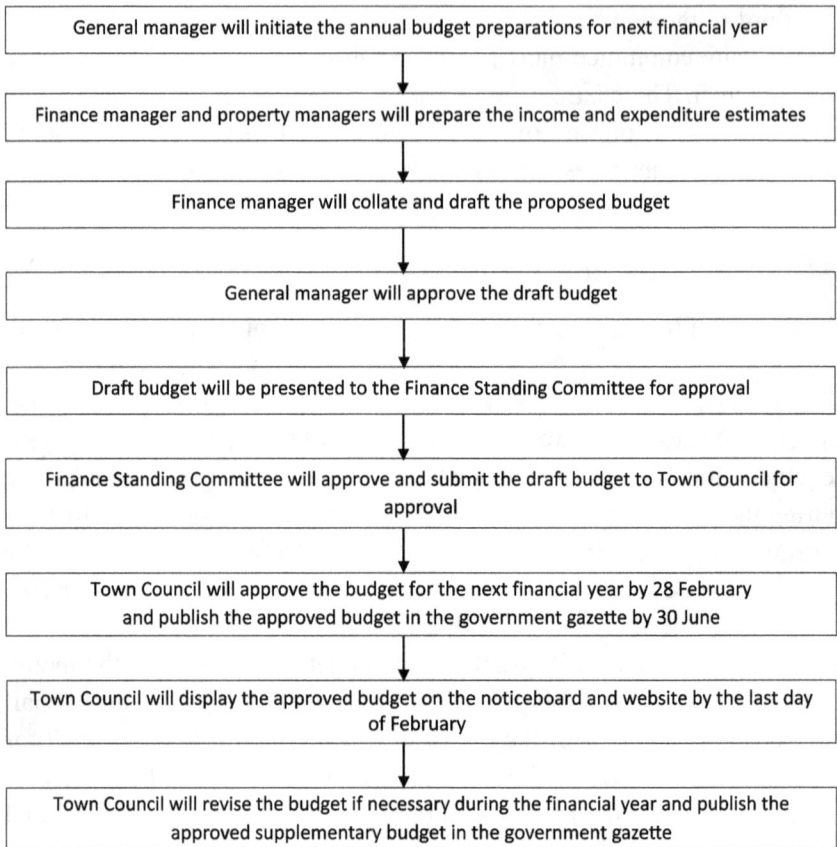

Figure 3.4   Budget Preparation for Town Council

Table 3.1   Income and Expenditure Budget Statement (FY XX/XX+1)

	Actual (FY XX/XX+1)	Budget (FY XX+1/XX+2)	Variance ($) (%)	Remarks
Operating income				
Service & Conservancy Charges (S&CC)				
Less operating income transfer to sinking fund				
S&CC after transfer to sinking fund				
Car park operating income				

Table 3.1 (*Continued*)

	Actual (FY XX/XX+1)	Budget (FY XX+1/XX+2)	Variance ($) (%)	Remarks
Other income				
Total income				
Less				
Operating expenditure				
Cleaning expenses				
Managing Agent fees				
Lift maintenance				
Repair and maintenance expenses				
Utilities expenses				
General & administrative expenditures				
Total expenditure				
Operating surplus/(deficit)				
Add				
Non-operating income				
Investment & interest				
Surplus/(Deficit) before taxation and government grants				
Less				
Taxation				
Surplus/(Deficit) before government grants				
Add				
Government grant				
Less transfer to sinking fund				
GST subvention grant				
Less transfer to sinking fund				
Surplus/(Deficit) after government grants				

(d) Determining the income from other sources such as rental of common property, TOL, use of electricity and water, investment and interest income, penalty and fines, sale of tender documents, subletting of office (if any), government grants and others.

The expenditure estimates will entail the following tasks:

(a) Conducting estate condition survey to determine the routine and replacement works to be carried out in the next financial year.
(b) Estimating the expenditure for term contracts such as managing agent fees, conservancy works, horticulture works, lift maintenance works, building works, sanitary works, mechanical and electrical works, etc. based on the term contract prices or schedule of rates for the next financial year.
(c) Estimating the general and administration expenditures for the town council office.
(d) Estimating the expenditures for utilities.
(e) Estimating the expenditures for activities relating to publicity and public relations.
(f) Estimating the expenditures for cyclical maintenance works scheduled for the next financial year, including the project management and consultancy fees.
(g) Estimating the expenditures for town improvement and upgrading projects.
(h) Estimating the capital expenditures for the additions of new assets or replacement of existing assets, such as office renovation, furniture and fittings, office equipment or data processing equipment.

The proposed budget will be approved by the town council and will be displayed on the town council's noticeboard and website by the last day of February. Thereafter, the town council will publish the approved budget in the government gazette by 30th June. Data from the approved budget will be stored in the Town Council Management System (TCMS) for monitoring and reporting purposes as work progresses. It is common for town councils to review and revise their budget in the middle of the financial year to better reflect changes in income or expenditure patterns. A supplementary budget can also be approved due to unforeseen circumstances, such as change in town council's boundaries or portfolio of flats, revision of S&CC rates and emergency works. The revised budget shall be approved by council and gazetted accordingly.

Chapter 4

Routine Maintenance Management

4.1 Introduction

The main purpose of the town council is to ensure the Housing and Development Board (HDB) estates are in a clean and serviceable condition. As such, various types of routine maintenance works have to be carried out at different frequencies to attain the maintenance standards set. These routine maintenance works are usually performed by term contractors who will schedule their works according to the requirements of the term contracts, such as daily sweeping and refuse collection, weekly bin chute flushing, fortnightly grass-cutting, monthly block washing, quarterly fumigation of bin chutes, half-yearly servicing of electrical installations and yearly water tank flushing and sanitation.

Upon the submission of the routine maintenance work schedules by various term contractors, the town council will plan out a master routine maintenance programme. This information can then be keyed into a computer system to plan out the weekly or monthly inspection schedules for the property managers and officers. The inspection schedules can be digitised and made available via smartphone to facilitate access by the property officers. In this way, the property officers can inspect different parts of the buildings and estates more systematically and comprehensively and, at the same time, attend to complaints and feedback from residents and stakeholders.

4.2 Types and Scope of Routine Maintenance Work

The types of routine maintenance work of a town include the following:

(a) **Conservancy and cleaning work**: This work comprises the routine conservancy and cleaning works that are carried out on a daily basis including Sundays and public holidays. These include dry sweeping, mopping and disinfection of common corridors of blocks, staircases, lifts, void decks, open spaces, footpaths, carparks, drains and amenities in the estates. Daily clearing of bins and refuse collection including washing of bin centres and centralised refuse chute system are also carried out. The town council will also provide weekly free bulky items removal for residents and removal of any obstructions at the common property which may pose safety hazards and maintenance problems. In addition, monthly block washing is carried out to ensure that all blocks are kept in a clean and hygienic condition. The performance standard for cleaning is based on the Singapore Standard SS 533: 2007.

(b) **Grass-cutting, horticulture and arboriculture work**: This work comprises the cutting and maintenance of grass in parks, open spaces and carparks in the town. It includes the trimming of grass and vegetation along edges of tracks, footpaths, drains, between footpath slabs, in spaces of perforated slabs, beside park furniture, installations and structures, removal of weeds and clearing of cut grass and debris. Grass-cutting is usually carried out fortnightly, bi-monthly or every five months depending on the types of grass. The performance standard set for grass after the cutting is as follows:

- Axonopus compressus (cow grass) — 10 to 20 mm
- Zoysia matrella (carpet grass) — 5 to 15 mm
- Axonopus sp. (pearl grass) — 10 to 15 mm

As for horticulture work, it consists of the maintenance of shrubs, hedges, foliage, turf areas and vegetation in the town on a monthly basis. The performance standard set for horticulture work is that the trees, shrubs, hedges, turf areas and vegetation must be kept healthy and free from pests and diseases.

(c) **Building tradesmen work**: This work comprises minor building repairs, rectification of building defects, alteration and addition works in the town. Work orders are usually issued by the property officers for building tradesmen works. These include rectifying water seepages, repairing cracks and spalling concrete, repair/replacement of building components and amenities, such as railings, false ceilings, benches, doors, footpaths, re-screeding of building apron or retiling of floor. The performance standard set is with reference to various Singapore Standards, Codes of Practice and other recognised international building standards for various building trades.

(d) **Sanitary, plumbing, and water tank work**: This work comprises the washing, cleaning, flushing, repainting and sterilisation of water tanks to comply with relevant regulations requirements of the relevant authorities. It also includes the inspection, testing and repair of sanitary and plumbing works to comply with relevant building standards, code of practice and regulations by the authorities.

(e) **Electrical works and carpark lightings**: This work comprises the maintenance, repair, alteration and addition of lightings and electrical installations at the common property of residential and commercial property, carparks and estate amenities.

(f) **Inspection and testing of electrical installations**: This work comprises the inspection, maintenance and testing of electrical installations to comply with licensing requirements of the authorities. The work has to be carried out by a Licensed Electrical Worker.

(g) **Lift maintenance work**: This work comprises the monthly servicing and maintenance of lifts including the replacement of components and parts as and when necessary. It also includes lift rescue services for man-trapped cases, testing of lifts for statutory compliance and maintenance of the Automatic Rescue Device (ARD). The performance standard set is based on SS 550:2009 which specifies the 20 maintenance outcomes as required by the Building and Construction Authority. In addition, the lift performance is monitored based on the number of lift breakdowns as recorded in the Lift Telemonitoring System (LTMS) and complaints received as captured in the Integrated Estate Management System (IEMS).

(h) **Lift Surveillance System (LSS)**: This work comprises the provision of comprehensive maintenance to maintain the LSS, including checking its operational functionality. It includes the retrieval of video recordings for investigation and enforcement purposes.

(i) **Painting of road marks**: The work comprises the painting of service roads, driveways, surface carparks, multi-storey carparks, loading/unloading bays, parks, cycling/jogging tracks and passageways under the town council. This includes the painting of letterings in relation to all properties of the town.

(j) **Fire protection system work**: This work comprises the servicing, maintenance and testing of the fire protection installations and works.

(k) **Carpark, traffic and estate signs work**: This work includes the supply, delivery and installation of estate signboards, carpark and traffic signs in the town.

(l) **Pest control work**: This work comprises the inspection, extermination and eradication of white ants, beehives and other pests. Regular culling operations are also carried out to eradicate rodents and other pests.

(m) **Emergency Battery Operated Power Supply (EBOPS) work**: This work comprises the maintenance and testing of EBOPS to ensure its functionality.

(n) **Provision of Essential Maintenance Services Unit (EMSU)**: This work comprises the provision of a 24-hour hotline for town councils. The service includes call centre operations, emergency repairs and lift rescue services for man-trapped cases. The EMSU will receive complaints and feedback from residents and various stakeholders. These will be channelled to the town council management team, contractors or relevant government agencies for them to take the necessary follow-up action. The EMSU will provide monthly performance reports to the town council. The performance standard set for phone calls is that all calls must be answered within six rings by the operator. As for lift rescue, the time taken to release trapped persons shall not exceed 25 minutes from the time EMSU receives the feedback, unless the rescue work is beyond the capability of the lift operator.

(o) **Transfer and diverter pumps, booster pumps, submersible pumps and refuse chute flushing system work**: This work comprises the maintenance of all pump installations including refuse chute flushing system. It includes quarterly servicing of solenoid valves and annual tests for water flowrate for transfer pumps and annual cables insulation and continuity tests. The performance standard set is based on the requirements by the authorities.

(p) **Electrically or manually operated roller doors work**: This work comprises the maintenance, repair and replacement of parts for the electrically operated roller shutter door at centralised refuse chutes, bin compounds and utility centres of the town. Inspection is to be carried out once every six months to ensure that the roller shutter doors are in a good and usable condition.

(q) **Safety inspection of children's playground and fitness corner work**: This work comprises the physical safety inspection of childrens' playgrounds and fitness equipment in the town.

(r) **Refuse handling equipment work**: This work comprises the comprehensive maintenance of the refuse handling equipment (dust screw type of compactor) and includes the repair/replacement of parts to the equipment.

(s) **Mechanical fan and exhaust system work**: This work comprises the maintenance and servicing of mechanical fan and exhaust systems installed at various premises, such as basement carparks and hawker centres. Quarterly cleaning and maintenance are usually carried out to ensure that mechanical fan and exhaust systems are working properly and kept in a clean and serviceable condition.

(t) **Air-conditioning and ventilation system work**: This work comprises mainly the inspection, servicing, maintenance and rectification of faults, and replacement of parts of mechanical ventilation and air-conditioning systems at the town council offices and specified premises. Inspection and servicing are normally carried out monthly.

(u) **Water dispenser (car wash) work**: This work comprises the leasing of water dispensers to be installed at multi-storey carparks and car wash bays. The work includes the servicing and repair of the water dispensers to ensure functionality.

(v) **Alert Alarm System (AAS) work**: This work comprises the comprehensive maintenance of the AAS to ensure that it is in good working condition at all times. Preventive and corrective maintenance shall be carried out including attending to *ad-hoc* requests by residents to activate or deactivate the alarm within the residential unit.

(w) **Provision of enforcement and security services**: The work scope includes inspection and enforcement of both residential and commercial properties to ensure compliance with town council by-laws and relevant regulations, such as fire safety. This is to ensure that commercial shops display their goods within approved Outdoor Display Area (ODA) and residents do not clutter common corridors and staircase landings with bulky items, furniture or potted plants.

(x) **IEMS work**: The IEMS is a centralised computerised system which captures all complaints and feedback to the town councils through various channels, such as phone calls, site inspections, walk-ins, social media, municipal services office referrals, letters, and lift tele-monitoring system (LTMS). The LTMS tracks the performance of the lifts in terms of lift breakdowns, man-trapped, power failure alert, frequency and duration of maintenance. The IEMS has a dashboard to facilitate the monitoring and management of complaints/feedback. It also provides various management reports to monitor complaints/feedback trends and follow-up actions.

(y) **Estate supplies**: This term contract provides the purchase of commonly used estate supplies such as little bins, refuse bins, bulk bins and lift tubes based on a tendered schedule of rates.

(z) **Provision of security services**: This work comprises the provision of security officers to escort contractors and service providers to access the rooftop to carry out works. This is to ensure that there are no security breaches of the rooftop water tanks and other installations on the roof.

4.3 Term Contracts for Routine Maintenance Work

In the town council, a large proportion of the work entails the routine maintenance of buildings, common property and amenities in the town. Routine maintenance works are usually outsourced by the town council on a term contract basis. These works are packaged according to the different building trades. Term contractors are engaged to provide the services for a specified period of time (term contract duration) and at an agreed price (tendered price) based on open tender. The town council will specify the requirements for various types of routine maintenance works based on the manufacturers' recommendations, statutory compliance or town council's requirements. These routine maintenance work term contracts typically last for 2–3 years as this ensures continuity of services whilst concurrently allowing the term contractors to enjoy economies of scale and to pass on these cost advantages to the town council in the form of a lower quote. The list of term contracts for routine maintenance work is as follows:

(a) **Building and estate maintenance work**
- building tradesmen works;
- sanitary, plumbing works and water tanks;
- electrical works and carpark lightings;
- inspection and testing of electrical installations (licensing purpose);
- conservancy and cleaning works;
- grass-cutting, horticulture and arboriculture works;
- lift maintenance;
- lift surveillance system;
- painting of road marks;
- fire protection system;
- carpark/traffic/estate signs;
- pest control;
- Emergency Battery Operated Power Supply (EBOPS);
- transfer and diverter pumps, booster pumps, submersible pumps and refuse chute flushing system;
- inspection and testing of electrical installations work;
- provision of Essential Maintenance Services Unit (EMSU) (24 hours);
- electrically or manually operated roller doors;
- refuse handling equipment;
- mechanical fan and exhaust system;
- air-conditioning and ventilation system;
- water dispenser (car wash);
- Alert Alarm System (AAS);
- safety inspection of children's playground and fitness corner;
- provision of enforcement and security services; and
- Integrated Estate Management System (IEMS).

(b) **Estate supplies**
  • supply and delivery of estate bins; and
  • supply and delivery of light tubes/starters/compact lamps.
(c) **Office administration**
  • Town Council Computer Management System (TCMS);
  • fire insurance;
  • theft insurance;
  • money insurance;
  • public liability insurance;
  • supply and delivery of office stationery; and
  • supply, printing, pressure sealing and mailing of standard letter.
(d) **Others**
  • design, print and delivery of town council newsletters;
  • appointment of consultants (architects, project managers, quantity surveyors);
  • agreement for lift monitoring services (telemonitoring system); and
  • agreement for routine maintenance of HDB parking places.

As for the managing agent's contract, the town council will normally prefer to have a longer contract duration of about 4 or 5 years with a further option to extend the contract for 1 or 2 years. This will help to reduce any disruption of town council services when there is a change of managing agent, especially near the General Elections. In Singapore, General Elections are held within 5 years after the last election. After every General Election, there may be changes to the boundary of the town and its portfolio of HDB flats and shops. The incumbent managing agent will then be responsible for ensuring a smooth handover of the town to the newly formed town council. The handover can sometimes be complex when the handover takes place between or among different elected Members of Parliament (MPs) of different political parties.

4.4 Maintenance Policies and By-laws

Based on the portfolio of HDB residential and commercial properties and the needs of the residents, the town council will formulate various maintenance policies and by-laws to control, manage, maintain and upgrade the estate. SOPs are usually developed to facilitate the implementation of maintenance policies and by-laws. The list of maintenance policies and by-laws of a town council is as follows:

(a) **Maintenance policies**

(i) **Financial policies**: The financial policies must be aligned with the Town Councils Act, Town Councils Financial Rules and directives or guidelines from the Ministry of National Development. The financial policies will entail the setting up of the finance standing committee, financial mandate for authorised personnel (town council chairperson, vice-chairpersons, secretary, finance committee chairperson, finance manager and managers), review of service and conservancy charges and other charges for the use of common property, internal controls for budget allocation and expenditure, arrears management, investment of town council funds, checks and balances measures for corporate governance, and risk management systems for business continuity.

(ii) **Procurement policies**: The procurement policies shall abide by the Town Councils Financial Rules in the procurement of goods and services for the council. This includes determining the "mandate of authority" as approved by the town council for the town council chairperson, tender committee, town council secretary, and managers in procuring goods and services for the town council. The tender committee shall be responsible for the approval of tender specifications, calling of tender, evaluating the tender and making recommendations to the council for the award of tenders. The tender committee may adopt different policies to ensure that the procurement process is open, transparent and fair to all bidders. This is to ensure that the town council's procurement represents good value for money and is publicly accountable for the prudent use of its funds.

(iii) **Estate management policies**: The estate management policies are usually formulated in tandem with the town council by-laws. The policies shall include Temporary Occupation Licence (TOL) terms, conditions and charges for the use of common property, shops' outdoor display areas, and display of goods during festive seasons, enforcement for infringements of by-laws, personal data protection and information management, tender policies (outcome-based tender specifications and Price Quality Method for tender evaluation), and standards of routine maintenance works.

(iv)   **Upgrading of estate policies**: The policies and guidelines for HDB upgrading programmes are stipulated by the HDB. These policies usually specify the criteria for eligibility for various types of upgrading programmes and cost-sharing basis for the upgrading cost among the government, town council and residents or shop owners. Besides HDB upgrading programmes, the town council will also implement various upgrading and town improvement projects. The council may set policies for the allocation of funding for such projects among the political divisions or formulate policies to guide the implementation of town improvement projects to fulfil the vision and mission of the town.

(b) Town Council by-laws

In order to ensure proper housekeeping and encourage socially responsible habits among its residents, shop operators and the general public, the town council has often empowered its officers to take enforcement action against those who infringe the by-laws. The by-laws are usually made by the town councils to address the following problems:

(i)   **Dumping and renovation debris**: The by-laws are intended to prevent the illegal dumping of renovation debris by contractors, residents or others during renovation works. Residents who renovate their flats must obtain the approval of HDB to engage a HDB-licensed contractor to carry out the works and abide by the HDB's and town council's rules and by-laws. The renovation contractor is responsible for the proper disposal of renovation debris. These are necessary because the illegal dumping of debris or things at common areas could potentially become a safety or fire hazard.

(ii)   **Obstruction of common property**: The by-laws are intended to prevent residents or shop operators from placing objects, things or fixtures that will obstruct the use of common property. A perennial problem faced by town councils is the obstruction of the common corridor by residents and shop operators. Examples of objects that tend to obstruct the common corridor include shoe racks, potted plants, cabinets, furniture, bicycles, commercial goods, recyclables, clothes racks, and religious artefacts.

(iii) **Damage to common property**: The by-laws are intended to prevent any person from damaging or removing common property. A common problem faced by town councils is the damage caused to lift doors and ceilings due to the transportation of materials and goods.

(iv) **Misuse of common property and open spaces**: The by-laws are intended to prevent residents from misusing common property, such as by bathing, swimming or fishing in ponds or fountains.

(v) **Damage to turf, plant, shrub or tree**: The by-laws are intended to prevent residents, shop operators, contractors and the general public from removing or damaging any turf, plant, shrub or tree at common property. This also includes unauthorised planting of trees or shrubs at the common property. Very often, event organisers or trade fair operators also cause damage to the turf or trees when organising events in open spaces. As such, they are required to rectify any damage caused to the turf or trees after the event.

(vi) **Illegal parking**: The by-laws are intended to prevent illegal driving, riding or parking of cars, motorcycles or motorised vehicles at the common properties as this might obstruct the use of the common property and pose a safety hazard to others. As the common properties are frequently used by residents, vehicles are not to be driven in these locations, unless for emergency purposes.

(vii) **Power to detain or remove vehicle**: The by-laws empower the town council to detain or remove any vehicle infringing the by-law.

4.5 Estate Inspection System (EIS)

The Estate Inspection System provides a systematic approach for scheduling estate inspections and appointments. It provides a standardised and comprehensive format to keep records of physical inspections and maintenance follow-up actions by the property officers. As the portfolio and block design of residential and commercial properties of each town is different, the town council will have to map out the most efficient approach for its property officers to inspect the estates productively and efficiently. Areas with higher human or vehicular traffic are usually inspected more frequently for safety reasons. These include town centres, hawker centres, common corridors, void decks, footpaths, communal amenities and parks. In a town, each property manager is usually assigned to manage a division or constituency and support the elected MP. Every property manager will supervise a team of property officers who will each manage about 20–30 blocks of residential and commercial units. Each property officer will divide the total number of blocks into four batches comprising about 4–6 blocks per batch. Each batch of blocks will be inspected comprehensively over four weeks with four different areas of focus. The key areas of focus for the inspection include:

(a) **Building Detail (BD)**: detailed inspection of building areas, such as every common corridor, staircase, centralised refuse chute hopper, lift landing, lift car, void deck, building apron and surface drain;
(b) **Building non-accessible (BN)**: detailed inspection of non-accessible areas to the general public, such as roof, water tank room, lift motor room, electrical switch room, and pump room;
(c) **Building General (BG)**: random inspection of building areas as listed in BD and BN; and
(d) **Ground General (GG)**: inspection of open spaces, amenities, landscape areas, trees, surface carpark and multi-storey carparks.

Table 4.1 shows a typical inspection schedule for a property officer for the purposes of inspecting the estate. The EIS process is shown in Figure 4.1.

4.6 Integrated Estate Management System (IEMS)

The IEMS is a computerised system which collects data from the feedback and suggestions from residents and stakeholders (Figure 4.2). It will

Table 4.1 Inspection Schedule for Estate Inspection

Working Days	Week 1	Week 2	Week 3	Week 4
Monday	Batch 1 (BD, BN, BG)	Batch 1 (BD, BN, BG)	Batch 1 (BD, BN, BG)	Batch 1 (BD, BN, BG)
	Batch 1 & 2 (GG)	Batch 1 & 2 (GG)	Batch 1 & 2 (GG)	Batch 1 & 2 (GG)
Tuesday	Batch 3 (BD, BN, BG)	Batch 3 (BD, BN, BG)	Batch 3 (BD, BN, BG)	Batch 3 (BD, BN, BG)
	Batch 3 & 4 (GG)	Batch 3 & 4 (GG)	Batch 3 & 4 (GG)	Batch 3 & 4 (GG)
Wednesday	Batch 2 (BD, BN, BG)	Batch 2 (BD, BN, BG)	Batch 2 (BD, BN, BG)	Batch 2 (BD, BN, BG)
	Batch 1 & 2 (GG)	Batch 1 & 2 (GG)	Batch 1 & 2 (GG)	Batch 1 & 2 (GG)
Thursday	Batch 4 (BD, BN, BG)	Batch 4 (BD, BN, BG)	Batch 4 (BD, BN, BG)	Batch 4 (BD, BN, BG)
	Batch 3 & 4 (GG)	Batch 3 & 4 (GG)	Batch 3 & 4 (GG)	Batch 3 & 4 (GG)
Friday	Reserved for make-up inspection			

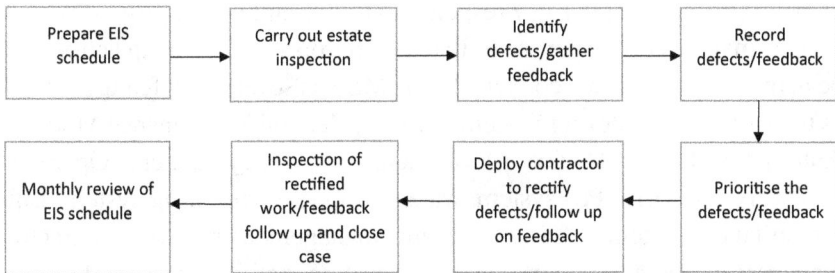

Figure 4.1 Estate Inspection System

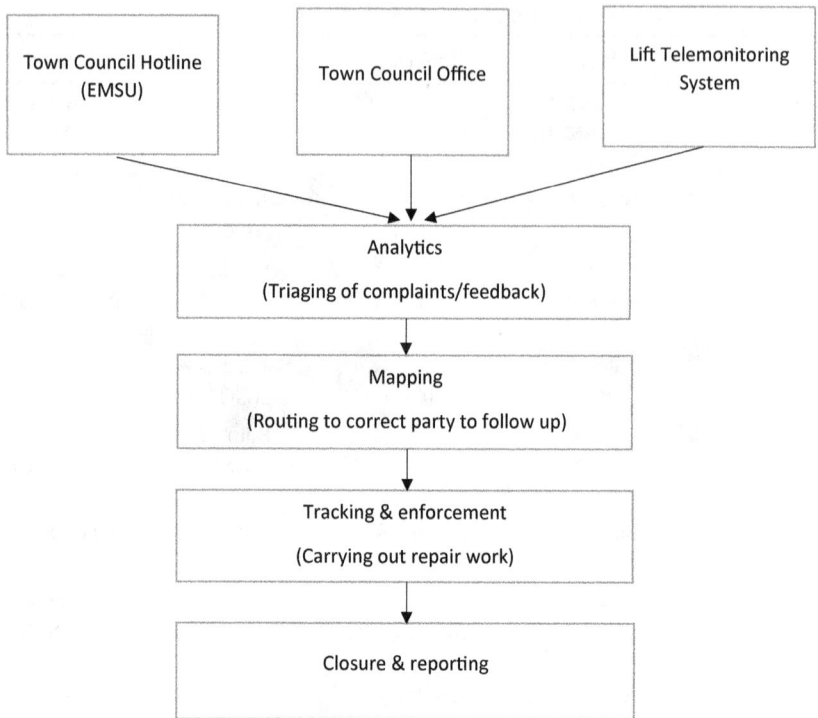

Figure 4.2   Integrated Estate Management System (IEMS)

triage and prioritise the feedback received into different classifications, namely, (i) immediate (1 day response), (ii) urgent (3 days response), and (iii) normal (7 days response) so that the appropriate follow-up action can be activated by the town council. The IEMS has several key features, such as the Lift Telemonitoring System (LTMS), General Maintenance Module, Automatic Rescue Device (ARD) and Emergency Battery Operated Power System (EBOPS) system, water pump telemonitoring system, Lift Surveillance System (LSS), call centre management module, contractor management module, report generation system, and integrated SMS notification system.

The TMS provides real-time monitoring of lift performance. It has a Lift Monitoring Device (LMD) which is connected to specific parts of the lift equipment so as to tap the respective signals for automatic lift fault detection. The LMD is connected to over 30 lift interface points which help to monitor 18 critical lift faults for instantaneous reporting to the lift firms and Essential Maintenance Service Unit (EMSU). The LTMS facilitates the rescue of individuals trapped in lifts and monitors the rectification process of lift breakdowns so as to reduce the downtime. As for the ARD and EBOPS, remote testing is conducted monthly to ensure that both the ARD and EBOPS are functional. When there is a power failure, the ARD and EBOPS will be activated to bring the lift cage with passengers to the nearest lift landing and open the door for passengers to evacuate.

The water pump telemonitoring system tracks the performance of the pump system in areas, such as power faults, emergency and alarm start alerts, pump trips alerts, roof tank as well as suction tank pump overflow or low-level alerts and duty pump failure alerts. The LSS provides video recordings of the lift cage and deters crime and vandalism. The call centre management module logs in all feedback received from residents and stakeholders through various channels, such as by word of mouth, site inspections, emails, LTMS, and Municipal Services Office's One Service Mobile Application. The town council will then be able to monitor the feedback and its follow-up actions through the IEMS. Authorised town councillors and officers will then also be able to monitor trends and records of the feedback and the follow-up actions through the IEMS dashboard.

The contractor management module allows the town council to channel feedback directly to contractors so that they can undertake rectification works as soon as possible. With the IEMS mobile application, contractors will also be able to receive feedback and further instructions relating to the work to be done from town council instantaneously. Upon completion of the work, the contractor will report the status of work to the town council through the IEMS mobile application, thus enabling the property officer to close the cases accordingly. The report generation module also allows the town council to generate various operational reports to monitor feedback trends, status of follow-up actions taken, ageing report for cases, and information for town council meetings. The integrated SMS notification system allows feedback to be routed to property officers and contractors to expedite follow-up actions.

The IEMS dashboard management system provides real-time information of the complaints received and the status of follow-up actions taken so that the town council can monitor its performance on service

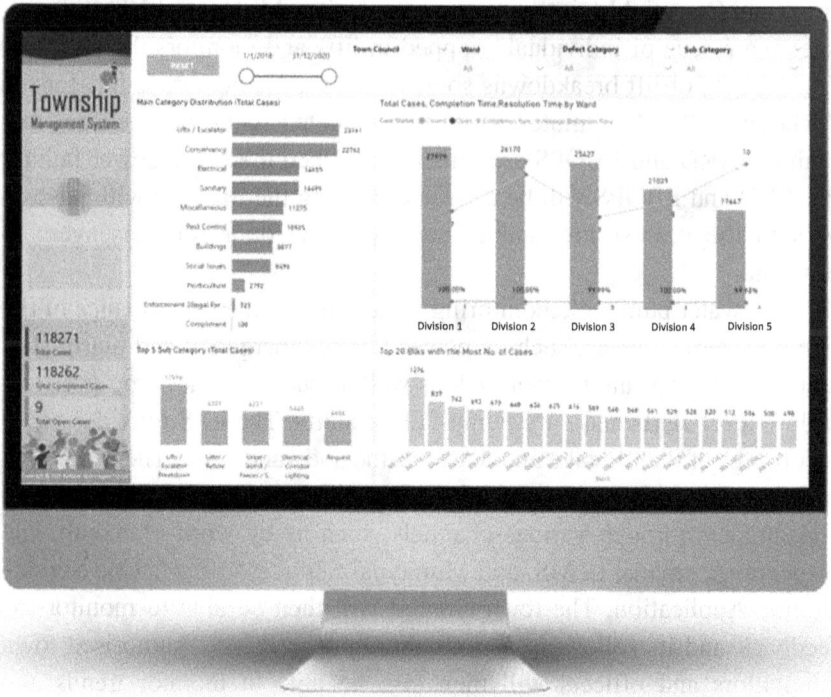

Figure 4.3   IEMS Dashboard Management System
Source: Surbana Technologies Pte Ltd

delivery. The dashboard is accessible through mobile devices, such as smartphones and laptops. Figure 4.3 shows the information retrieved through the dashboard management system. Trends and data analysis can be performed to support management in formulating policies and allocating resources to improve the services of the town council.

4.7   Lift Dashboard Management System

The lift dashboard management system provides a one-stop information portal for the council and management team to identify key trends in the complaints or feedback received and lift breakdowns. It monitors the feedback relating to lifts from the LTMS and IEMS systems. From the data analytics, it can highlight the performance of both the lifts and lift firms. As shown in Figure 4.4, the lift dashboard will provide real-time

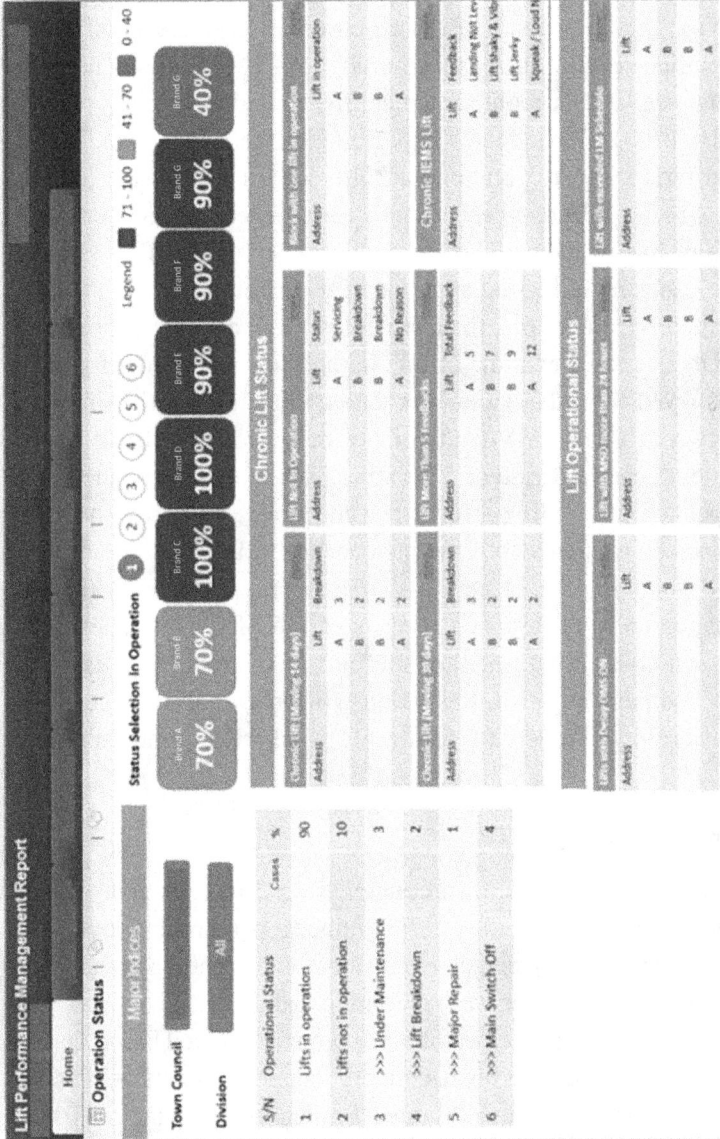

Figure 4.4   Lift Dashboard Management System

Source: Surbana Technologies Pte Ltd

information regarding the operational status of all lifts in the town, including those under repair or not operating. It also shows the number of lifts that are operational under each lift firm.

In addition, the number of lifts with chronic issues are highlighted based on specified criteria, such as the number of LTMS faults or number of complaints received per month for such lifts. Based on the past performance of the lifts and residents' expectations, the town council will specify the criteria to identify and monitor lifts with chronic issues in their respective towns. As a general rule, any lift which receives two or more LTMS faults or five or more IEMS complaints can be identified as a lift with chronic issues requiring the attention of the town council and the lift firms. By monitoring such lifts, the town council can channel appropriate resources to reduce the downtime of lifts in their towns. In order for such lifts to be removed from the list of lifts with chronic issues, the lift must not receive two or more TMS faults or not more than five IEMS complaints per month over a period of 5 months. The monitoring of such lifts has also helped to improve lift performance and reduce lift downtime, thus providing much convenience to residents over the years.

The lift dashboard management system also provides information on the performance and maintenance records of the lifts. From the dashboard, the town council can monitor the performance of the lifts from different lift companies. This information will provide useful feedback to HDB in awarding contracts for future lift installation in the estates.

4.8   Work Order System

The work order system of the town council is used for various types of routine maintenance contracts to carry out minor repair and improvement works, such as building repairs or mechanical and electrical repairs or replacement of parts. Under the various routine maintenance contracts, the schedule of rates for different types of work orders are listed based on the tender award rates. Thus, the town council property officers will issue work orders based on the schedule of rates. For works which are not listed in the term contract schedule of rates, the town council will either call quotations or use built-up rates to issue work orders.

(1) Feedback from residents and stakeholders.

(2) Property officer (PO) assesses the feedback and establishes the need to issue works order to contractor.

(3) PO conducts site visit to determine scope of work, take measurements and take pre-work photographs.

(4) PO prepares works order and seeks approval from PM/DGM/GM.

(5) Upon approval, PO issues works order to contractor.

(6) Upon completion of works, contractor will inform PO and submit post-work photographs.

(7) PO will check to ensure that work is properly done.

(8) PO will certify that work is completed accordingly to the works order.

(9) Contractor will send invoice for work done to Town Council for payment.

(10) PO will certify satisfactory completion of works, recommend payment and seek approval of PM/DGM/GM.

(11) PM/DGM/GM will approve payment of work and send to Finance department to process payment.

(12) Town Council will make payment to the contractor for works done.

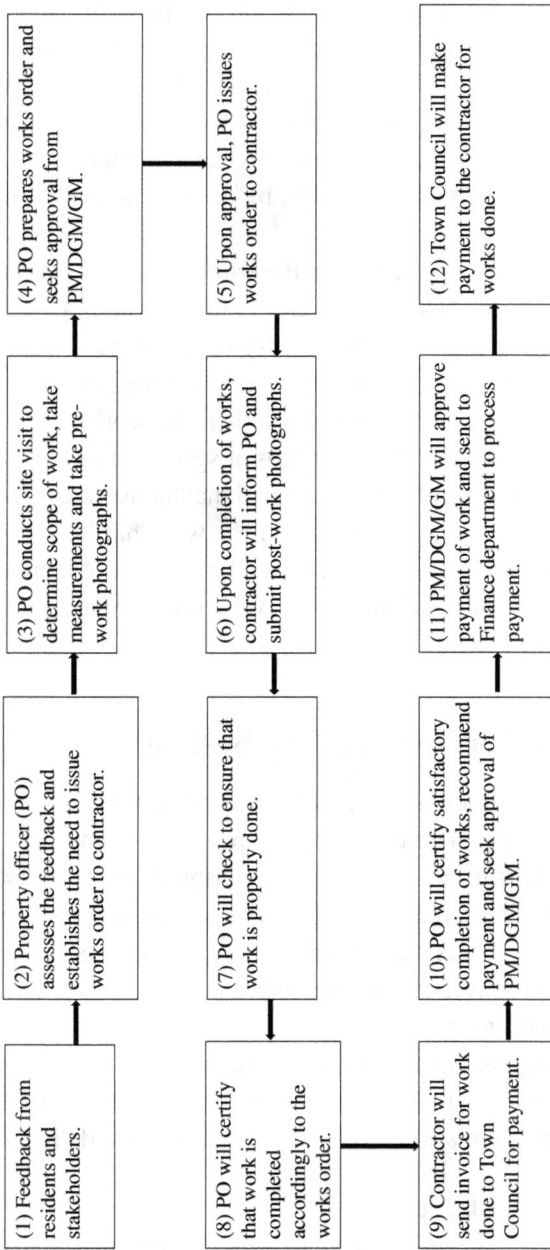

Figure 4.5   Work Order System

The need to undertake minor repairs or improvement works can either arise from the estate inspections conducted by property officers and managers or from feedback received from various stakeholders, such as MPs, town councillors, residents, government agencies or partners. Upon receiving the feedback, the property officers will first investigate the site, determine the requirements of the works, and take measurements (i.e. taking pre-work photographs), if necessary, before issuing the work order to the term contractor.

Once the term contractor receives the work order, the contractor will mobilise its workers and resources to carry out the works. Upon completion of the works, the contractor will notify the property officer and submit a report on the work done with post-work photographs. The property officer will then follow up to check whether the work has been done according to the issued work order in terms of specifications, quantity, and quality. Once the property officer is satisfied that the work has been properly carried out, he or she will certify that the work has been completed. Thereafter, the contractor will be able to send an invoice to claim payment for the work done. The workflow of a work order system is shown in Figure 4.5.

4.9   Customer Service Delivery System

Customer service is about building good relationships with residents and stakeholders of a town. The town council provides a range of township management services to meet the needs and aspirations of various stakeholders of a town. These include MPs, town councillors, residents, community leaders, merchants, and government agencies. As the customers and stakeholders are diverse and have different expectations, it is crucial for the town council to develop an effective and efficient customer service delivery system to ensure that its services can satisfy its customers. Thus, different town councils have set up different types of customer service toolkits and SOPs to guide their staff in service delivery.

(a) Customer service lapses
In order to set up a customer service delivery system that assures delivery of quality services, the town council must identify the common

lapses of its service delivery. These service lapses can often be grouped into the following categories:

(i) **Unfriendly and unhelpful staff**: Staff are not friendly and lack empathy when engaging customers, especially residents.
(ii) **Slow response to feedback**: Town council takes a long time to respond to complaints and feedback.
(iii) **Poor follow-up and rectification of works**: Staff are not diligent in ensuring that rectification works are done properly and updating residents on the progress.
(iv) **Inability to resolve problems**: Staff lack competency and experience to resolve problems faced by residents.
(v) **Communication problems**: Staff are not able to communicate clearly and explain policies and procedures to residents.

(b) **Customer service contact points**

When delivering town council services, the town council representatives (MPs, town councillors, and staff) will engage different stakeholders through different channels or platforms. The key customer service contact points of a town council are as follows:

(i) **Town council office walk-in counter (during office hours)**: Some residents, especially senior citizens, prefer to provide feedback to the town council personally at the town council office. In some instances, they request to see the property manager if feedback has not been addressed to their satisfaction.
(ii) **Essential Maintenance Service Unit (24 hours hotline)**: The town council usually outsources the hotline service to a call centre which will provide call services and emergency response works, such as lift rescues, emergency repairs of mechanical and electrical works, restoration of utilities and sanitary repairs.
(iii) **Town council call centre (during office hours)**: The town council call centre is usually managed in-house by its staff. The call centre will receive feedback from residents and stakeholders daily during office hours. The feedback will be logged into the IEMS so that follow-up actions can be taken.

(iv) **Town council website, Facebook, and Instagram**: The town council website provides information to keep residents updated on the happenings in the town. Town councils will also publish their annual reports and financial statements on the website for public scrutiny. This is to ensure public accountability of the use of town council funds. The town council website, Facebook and Instagram are all useful engagement platforms to encourage participation among residents in the management of the town.

(v) **MP site visits**: MPs often visit the blocks and estates of their respective constituencies to gather feedback and suggestions from residents on municipal issues. Such feedback may pertain to issues about cleanliness, safety, security, building defects, anti-social behaviour of residents, quality of work of town council staff and contractors, and suggestions for improvement projects.

(vi) **Property manager/officer estate inspection**: The property officers will conduct scheduled and *ad-hoc* inspections of their respective estates and meet up with residents and stakeholders regularly. Through site inspections and engagement of stakeholders, the town council will have first-hand knowledge of the needs and aspirations of the residents and stakeholders. This will help the town council to better specify the tender requirements so as to appoint suitable service providers to provide quality services for the residents.

(vii) **Media and social media channels**: Social media channels provide fast dissemination of information to residents, stakeholders and the general public on incidents or happenings in the town. This will either enhance or damage the image of the town council if the information or misinformation is not managed properly. Thus, the town councils have started using social media listening tools to alert town councils of online sentiment and potential issues which could go viral and impact the reputation of town councils. The town councils have also set up SOPs to better manage issues raised on social media.

(viii) **Contractors (conservancy, pest control, building, sanitary, M&E and enforcement service providers)**: Town council contractors providing different types of maintenance services will often come into contact with residents and various stakeholders. The town councils may thus require workers of these contractors to wear uniform so that they can be identified while working in the estates. Partnering with good contractors will help the town councils to improve the quality of services provided and build confidence among residents and stakeholders.

The key modes of service delivery at the above service contact points are as follows:

- face-to-face interactions;
- phone calls;
- emails, letters and social media postings;
- media channels; and
- through contractors and service providers.

(c) **Customer service qualities**
To continue delivering quality service through the various service contact points and modes of delivery, the town council must set up a quality assurance framework. The key attributes of good customer service are as follows:

(i) Staff must have a positive attitude.
(ii) Staff must be friendly, optimistic and patient.
(iii) Staff must listen to the customer's concerns attentively and be courteous and respectful when assisting them in resolving their issues.
(iv) Staff must have a good working knowledge of the Town Councils Act, Town Councils Financial Rules, By-laws, policies and procedures.
(v) Staff must be honest, helpful and fair when dealing with residents and stakeholders.
(vi) Staff must demonstrate a keenness to go the extra mile when serving residents and stakeholders.

(d) **Customer service toolkits**
Town councils have developed various customer toolkits to prepare their service contact points and staff and improve their quality of

service. The key components of a typical customer service toolkit are as follows:

   (i) professional grooming guidelines for staff (Table 4.2);
  (ii) customer-centric office setting (Table 4.3);
 (iii) professional etiquette (face-to-face engagement);
 (iv) professional etiquette (walk-in residents' engagement);
  (v) professional etiquette (telephone calls);
 (vi) professional etiquette (email and social media postings);
(vii) professional etiquette (print media); and
(viii) measurement of quality.

(i) Professional grooming guidelines for staff

Table 4.2 Professional Grooming Guidelines for Staff

For Women (Do's and Don'ts)		
S/No	**Do's**	**Don'ts**
1	Dress appropriately with minimal accessories.	Wearing revealing clothes.
2	Top is not too revealing and neatly tucked in or untucked.	Messy hair and scruffy shoes.
3	Light make-up for a simple fresh look.	Heavy make-up.
4	Maintain a fresh smell (mild perfume).	Strong perfume.
5	Keep nails clean and properly trimmed.	Dirty and chipped nail polish.
For Men (Do's and Don'ts)		
S/No	**Do's**	**Don'ts**
1	Wear clean, wrinkle-free shirt preferably in subtle colours, neatly tucked in or untucked and well-fitted trousers.	Wearing a crumpled shirt that is not properly tucked in and trousers that are too short.
2	Neat haircut and properly combed hair.	Messy and oily hair/nasal hair showing.
3	Shave regularly for a clean look.	Body odour and bad breath.
4	Apply a mild cologne.	Belt that looks really worn out.
5	Keep nails clean and properly trimmed.	Long and dirty nails.

(ii) **Customer-centric office setting**

Table 4.3   Customer-Centric Office Setting

S/No	Office Settings
1	Counter staff should wear proper uniform and name tag.
2	Reception counter should be clean, neat and uncluttered.
3	Customer waiting area should be clean, tidy and well lighted.
4	Reception office should be brightly lit with some greenery.
5	Reception entrance and area should be barrier-free with automatic sliding door.
6	Interview rooms should have glass partition and installed with CCTVs for security reasons.
7	Install a queue system with "counter serving" display screen visible to the waiting area.
8	Install clear directional signs in the office and display the operation hours prominently.
9	Install a noticeboard and display notices neatly for public viewing.
10	Place a suggestion box or digital service feedback system.

(iii) **Professional etiquette (face-to-face engagement)**
   Respect the customers
   - Be polite and friendly.
   - Greet residents with a warm smile.
   - Say 'Please' or 'Thank you' when asking residents for information.

   Focus on the customers
   - Find out what the resident's concerns and needs are.
   - Ask questions and listen to the resident's answers and observe his or her behaviour.
   - Show empathy and interest in the resident's concerns and needs.

   Go the extra mile and add a special touch
   - Focus on what is convenient for the residents and what would make them happy.
   - Explain your reasons when you have to say 'no' to their requests.
   - Let the residents know what his or her options are to create a personal touch.

Follow up and close the loop

- Staff should acknowledge receipt of the feedback to the resident within 24 hours either by speaking to them in person, calling them, emailing them or messaging them. For complex cases, staff should provide an interim reply to the resident that the case is being looked into and close the case within 3 days if possible.
- Close the loop by updating the resident once the case has been resolved.
- Thank the resident for providing the feedback.

(iv) **Professional etiquette (walk-in residents' engagement)**

- Greet the resident.
- Listen and engage the resident to find out more about the feedback.
- Assess the nature of the feedback.
- Record the case in the IEMS.
- Thank the resident for the feedback.
- Let the resident know that the town council will revert to them as soon as possible.

(v) **Professional etiquette (telephone calls)**

- Answer phone calls within three rings.
- Greet the resident.
- Introduce yourself and town council.
- Listen to the resident and find out more about the feedback.
- Assess the nature of the feedback.
- Record the case in the IEMS.
- Thank the resident for the feedback.

(vi) **Professional etiquette (email and social media postings)**

- Assess the nature of the feedback.
- Give an acknowledgement reply to the feedback provider.
- Record the case in the IEMS.
- If the case is not within the town council's jurisdiction, refer the case to the relevant agency for them to follow up.
- Update the resident and close the loop when the job has been successfully completed.

(vii) **Professional etiquette (print media)**
- Public Relations Manager (PRM) should monitor comments, public sentiment and the extent of distribution on the various media platforms.
- PRM should update the town council chairperson, GM and local MP on the developments.
- Record the case in the IEMS.
- PRM should respond to the media within five working days depending on the nature of the feedback and media queries.

(viii) **Measurement of service quality**

Town councils have implemented various methods to measure and monitor the quality of service for the purposes of continuous development. The key performance indicators for service quality are listed as follows:

- monthly complaint statistics from the IEMS (Figure 4.6);
- monthly random call survey to residents who provided feedback (Figure 4.7);

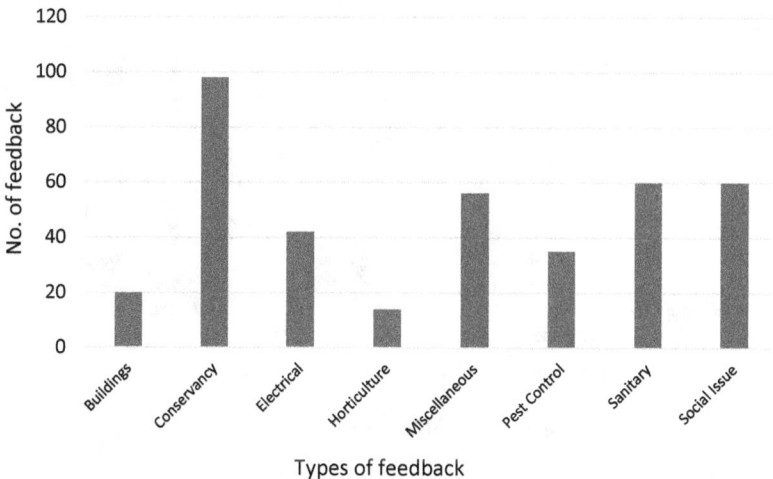

Figure 4.6   Monthly Statistics from the Integrated Estate Management System

How would you rate the overall services?
(Based on 100 Respondents)

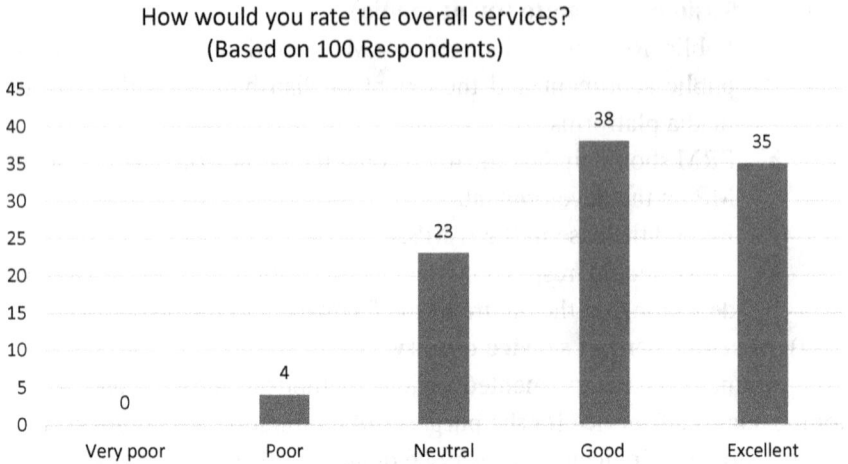

Figure 4.7   Monthly Random Call Survey

Number of feedback recorded and attended to within 7 days

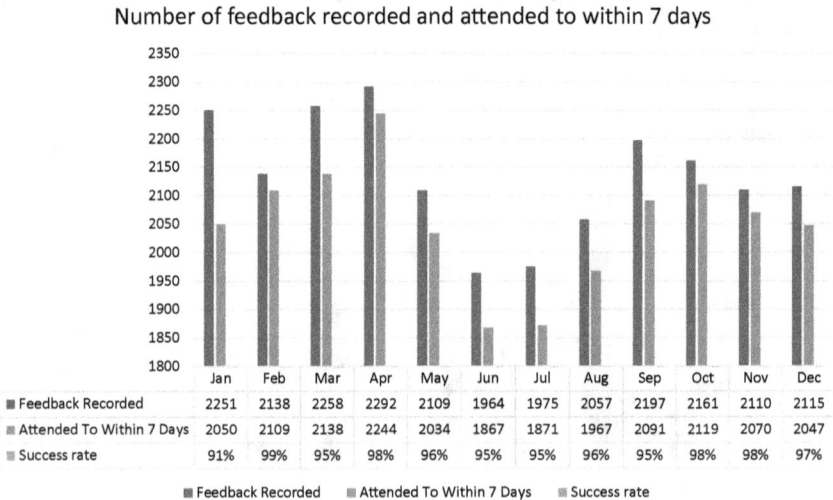

	Jan	Feb	Mar	Apr	May	Jun	Jul	Aug	Sep	Oct	Nov	Dec
Feedback Recorded	2251	2138	2258	2292	2109	1964	1975	2057	2197	2161	2110	2115
Attended To Within 7 Days	2050	2109	2138	2244	2034	1867	1871	1967	2091	2119	2070	2047
Success rate	91%	99%	95%	98%	96%	95%	95%	96%	95%	98%	98%	97%

■ Feedback Recorded   ■ Attended To Within 7 Days   ■ Success rate

Figure 4.8   Monthly Response Time

- monthly response time of feedback (Figure 4.8);
- number of compliments received (Figure 4.9);
- MP house visit report (Figure 4.10);

Number of compliments received for the period April 2019 to March 2020

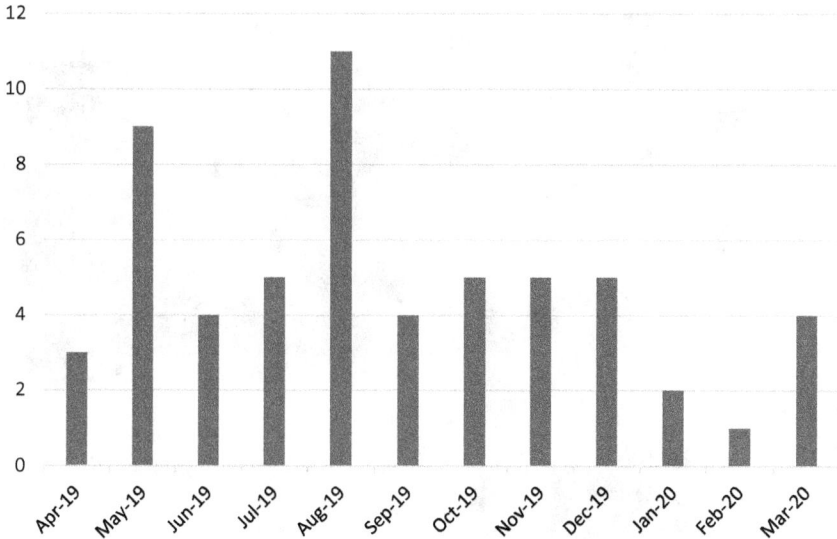

Figure 4.9   Number of Compliments

Block No: 400   Date: 24 August 2018   Time: 7.45PM

Total No. of Units: 110

Attended by: MP's name

S/N	Unit No.	Name	Telephone Number	Nature of Request/Complaint	Acion Taken	Completion Date
1	11-90	Ben		lift door open/closing too slow	refer to lift engineering to adjust speed	9/3/2018
2	06-66	Mr Tan		wet laundry/killer litter	notice served to advise residents	9/3/2018
3	04-34	Simon		high-rise littering	notice served to advise residents	9/3/2018
4	03-56	Ali		financial difficulty	recorded by CO staff	10/5/2018
5	02-23	Carl		financial difficulty	recorded by CO staff	10/5/2018
6	06-45	Mr Chan		neighbour smoking at the corridor	refer NEA	10/5/2018
7	06-77	Mr See		to install hump on the jogging path at the canal	refer to Nparks	10/5/2018
8	05-27	Mdm Soh		not enough incense burner	provide another incense burner	8/25/2018

Figure 4.10   MP House Visit Report

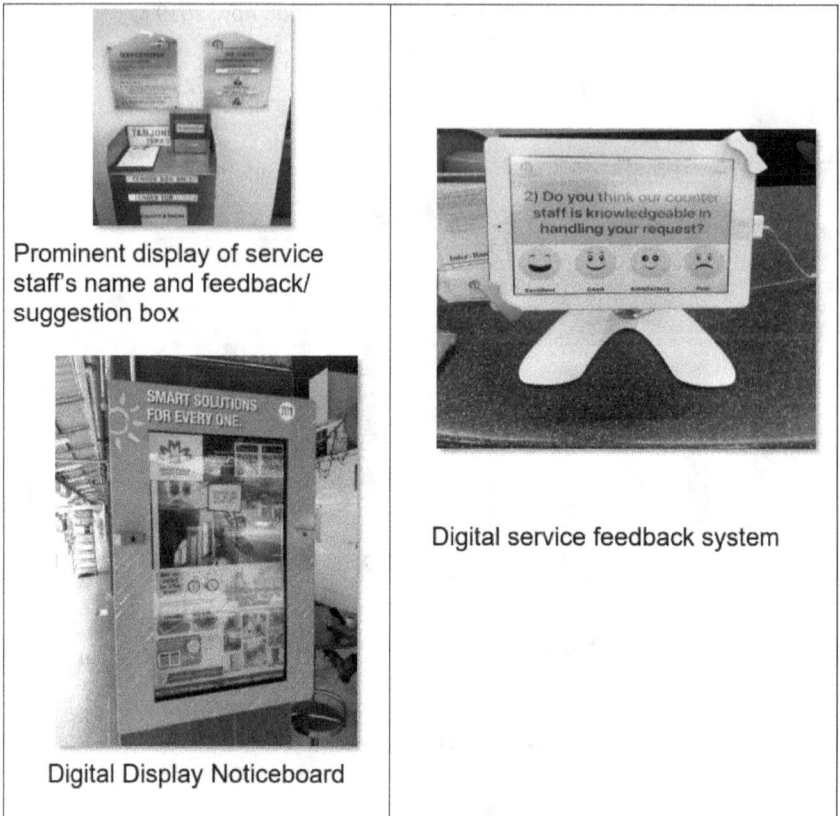

Prominent display of service staff's name and feedback/ suggestion box

Digital Display Noticeboard

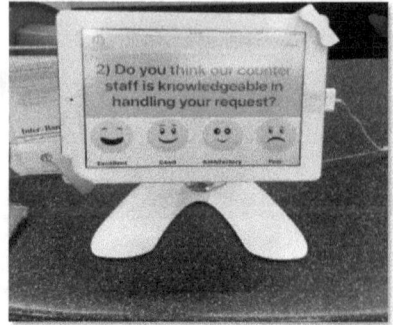

Digital service feedback system

Figure 4.11   Digital Feedback System

- digital feedback system at the reception counter (Figure 4.11);
- annual Town Council Management Report (Figure 4.12);
- annual customer service survey (Figure 4.13); and
- monthly customer service KPIs (Table 4.4).

FY2021 TCMR Operational Report
Results for Apr 2021 – Mar 2022

Town Council*	Estate Cleanliness	Estate Maintenance	Lift Performance	S&CC Arrears Management
Aljunied - Hougang				
Ang Mo Kio				
Bishan -Toa Payoh				
Chua Chu Kang				
East Coast				
Holland - Bukit Panjang				
Jalan Besar				
Jurong - Clementi				
Marine Parade				
Marsiling - Yew Tee				
Nee Soon				
Pasir Ris - Punggol				
Sembawang				
Sengkang				
Tampines				
Tanjong Pagar				
West Coast				

Figure 4.12   Annual Town Council Management Report

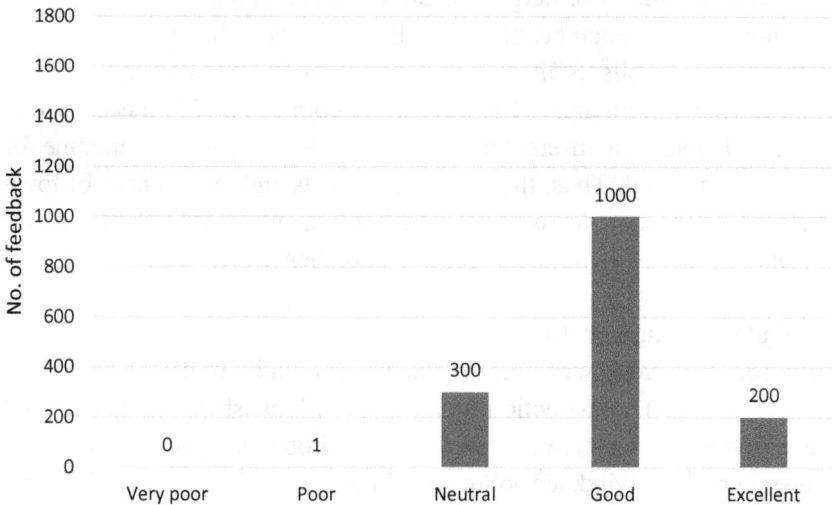

Figure 4.13   Annual Survey of Customer Service

Table 4.4 Monthly Customer Service KPIs

Performance Area	Current Performance Level	Tracking Mechanism and Control
Recording and attendance to maintenance feedback	96% of maintenance requests attended to within 7 days	• IEMS report • Work process to control
Deadline for replying to emails	• 100% interim reply • 90% replied within 7 days	• Mail registry • Work process to control
Deadline for replying to letters	90% replied within 7 days	• Mail registry • Work process to control
Deadline for reply to MP's letter	90% replied within 7 days	• Mail registry • Work process to control
Secret shopper	97% of shoppers have a "Happy" experience	• Secret shopper reports • Work process to control

4.10 Management of Complex Problems

Every year, the 17 town councils receive about one million feedback and complaints from their residents and stakeholders. Although the majority of the feedback and complaints are relatively simple to resolve, some complaints can be complex and thus require more time and resources to resolve. Examples of complex problems include water seepages, noise nuisances, obstructions, neighbour disputes, pet/animal nuisances, high-rise littering and mental health issues. Based on the collective experiences on the town councils, SOPs were set up to manage these complex problems, as shown in Figures 4.14–4.20. Every complex problem is unique in nature and requires a different approach to achieve a win–win outcome for all parties involved. Thus, the knowledge, skills and experiences of town council chairpersons, town councillors and management staff play a significant role in resolving these issues comprehensively.

(a) Water seepage problems

Water seepages can be attributed to the design (quality of design and selection of materials), construction (quality of workmanship), operations and usage (quality of maintenance services), environmental factors (sunlight, temperature, rain, wind, air pollutants or other chemicals) or wear and tear of the building components and materials. Water seepages usually happen either through external walls or from the rooftop to the upper-floor units (Figure 4.14). Thus, when seepages occur, especially for pre-fabricated blocks, the diagnosis of the seepages can be complex. The town council will normally work with HDB and waterproofing specialists to identify the cause of the seepage and implement appropriate rectification measures. However, the process may take some time, thus causing inconvenience and frustration to residents or stakeholders. The town council should take into consideration the following when managing water seepage cases:

- **Be responsive**: When the town council receives feedback or complaints on water seepages, it should respond immediately and contact the resident/shop operator to find out more details about the water seepages. The town council should also arrange for a site inspection with the resident/shop operator, and if necessary, invite an HDB officer or waterproofing specialist to be present.
- **Show empathy and seek understanding**: Show empathy to the resident/shop operator, especially if the water seepages have caused inconvenience or damaged the resident's/shop operator's property. Assure the resident/shop operator that the town council will conduct a thorough investigation to identify the source of the seepage and rectify the problem. Explain to the resident/shop operator that the investigation and repair may require some time due to its omplexity.
- **Communicate clearly**: Communicate clearly in simple terms to the resident/shop operator regarding the complexity of the water seepage problems. Keep the resident/shop operator updated on the proposed follow-up actions and progress of investigation and rectification works. Assure the resident/shop operator that you are paying close attention to the case to ensure that the works will progress smoothly, thus reducing further inconvenience to the resident. Do not raise expectations unnecessarily by promising the resident/shop operator that the problem will be resolved "as soon as possible" as it will likely result in disappointment.
- **Ensure safety and quality**: Make sure that safety measures are adopted when carrying out the investigation and rectification works. Ensure that occupants and workers are safe when carrying out the works within and outside the flat or shop. Take precautions to protect

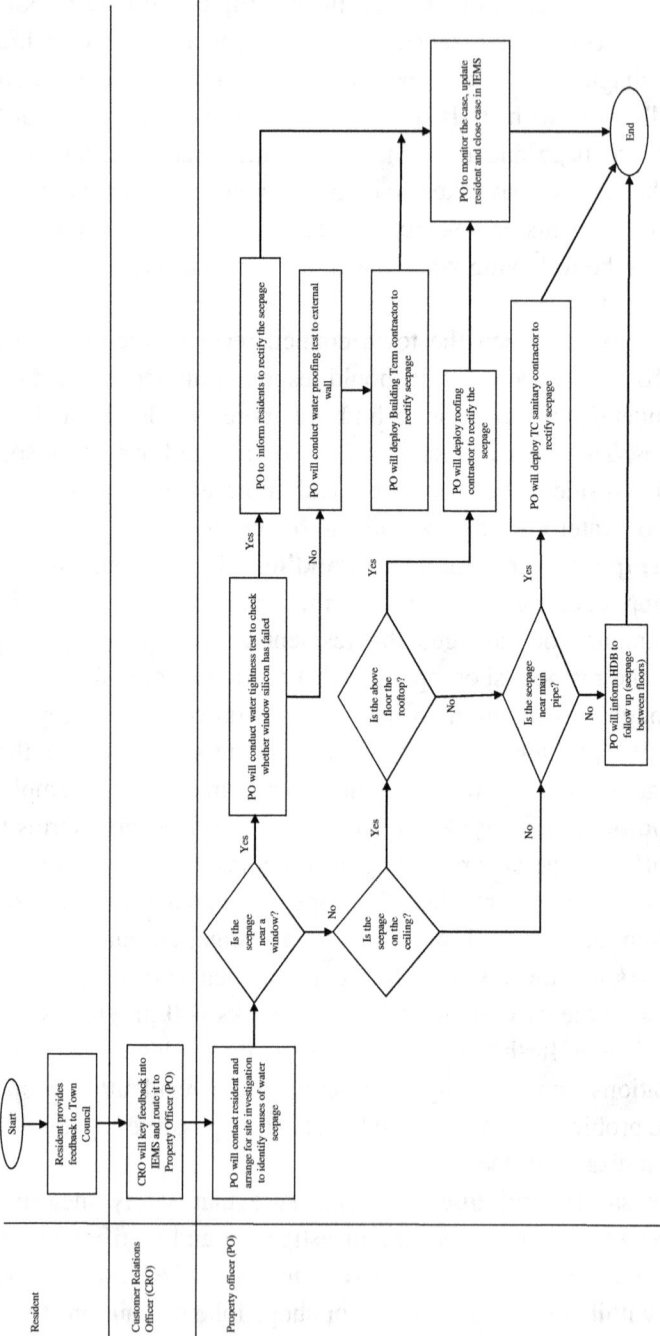

Figure 4.14 Flowchart for Water Seepage Problems

the property and belongings of the resident/shop operator within the premises. Make sure that the waterproofing specialist is doing a proper job to rectify the problems. Supervise the work closely.

- **Monitor case closely**: Monitor the progress of the case through the IEMS (ageing report status). Record the details of the follow-up actions taken. When the rectification work is completed, inform the resident/shop operator accordingly. Thereafter, monitor the case closely by checking with the resident/shop operator as to whether the water seepage has reoccurred.

(b) Noise nuisance problems

Noise nuisance caused by human/animal behaviour or activities within the flat or at the common property can be complex and may result in the wastage of town council resources when trying to find an amicable solution (Figure 4.15). HDB and town councils have rules and by-laws to ensure that residents and visitors live, work and play in a graceful and harmonious living environment. However, some residents or visitors do have anti-social habits that may cause noise nuisance to other residents. These problems may arise due to disputes between neighbours and rowdy gatherings at void decks or common areas, such as staircases or lift landings. The town council should take into consideration the following when managing noise nuisance cases:

- **Be responsive**: Respond quickly to the resident when a complaint of noise nuisance is received. Approach or contact the resident in a friendly manner, and find out more details about the noise nuisance. Go onsite to investigate the source of noise nuisance, especially if the noise nuisance occurs after office hours.
- **Show empathy**: Show empathy to the resident, especially if they have been badly affected by the noise nuisance and are suffering from lack of sleep, depression or just general frustration at the current situation they are in. Understand how the noise nuisance has affected the resident and his or her family members, and their expectations of how the issue should be resolved. If necessary, coordinate with HDB or other relevant agencies such as social service agencies or animal welfare societies to resolve the noise nuisance.

Start

Resident provides feedback to Town Council

CRO will key feedback into IEMS and route it to Property Officer (PO)

PO will contact resident to gather more information regarding the feedback

Is the noise nuisance from common property?

Yes → Noise nuisance occurred after 10.30pm?

No → PO will refer to HDB or relevant agencies to follow up

Yes → PO to refer the case to Police to follow up

No → PO will put up notice to advise residents to keep their volume down

PO to monitor the case, update resident and close case in IEMS

End

Resident

Customer Relations Officer (CRO)

Property officer (PO)

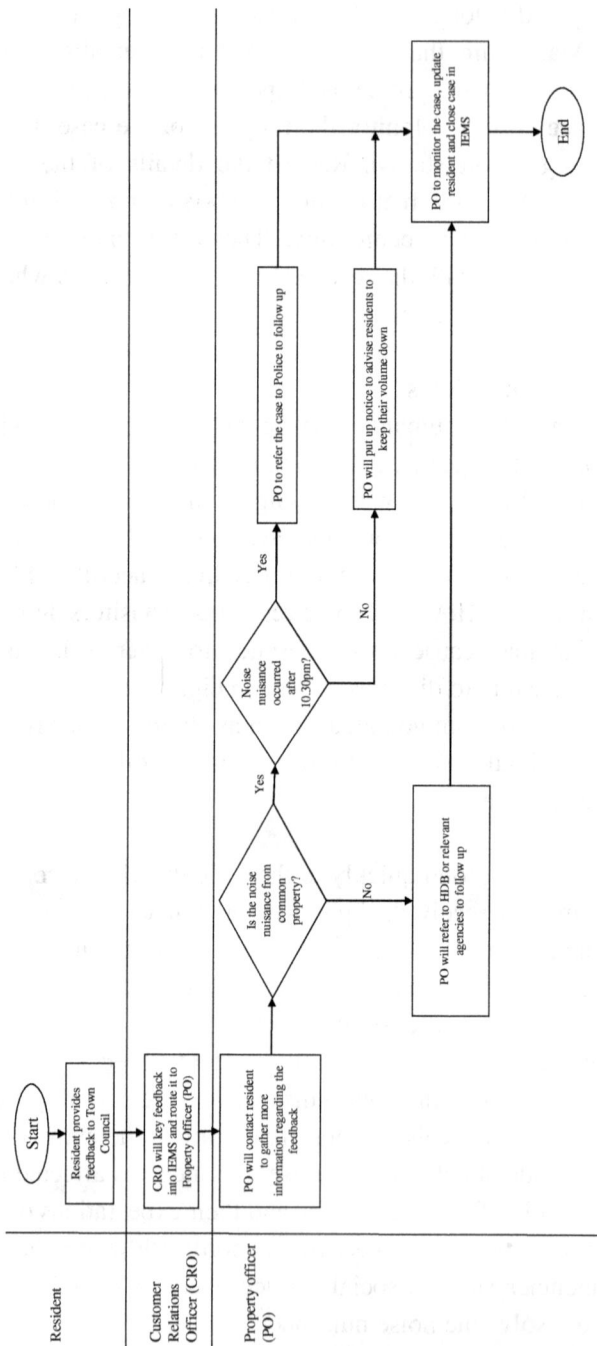

Figure 4.15 Flowchart for Noise Nuisance Problems

- **Communicate clearly**: Communicate clearly to the resident that you understand the nature of the noise nuisance and inform them of the follow-up actions to be taken to resolve the problem. If the problem is under another government agency's jurisdiction such as the HDB, police or National Environment Agency, coordinate with the agency to take appropriate measures or enforcement action, if necessary.
- **Monitor case closely**: Monitor the case closely by keeping in touch with the resident to ensure that the noise nuisance problem is resolved. If the noise nuisance persists, consider other options to resolve the problem, such as community mediation for disputes between neighbours, court injunctions to stop anti-social acts, or removal of seating facilities at void decks that attract rowdy gatherings.

(c) **Obstruction problems**

Obstructions along common corridors and staircase landings can pose a fire and safety hazard (Figure 4.16). This may result in injuries, loss of lives, or damage to property. Obstructions at the common property also prevents the town council from carrying out maintenance works, such as cleaning and washing. Residents tend to place many things along the common corridor and staircase landings of their flats. These items include potted plants, drying racks, cabinets, furniture, stores, bicycles, recyclables, and other bulky items. The town council will usually advise residents to practise good housekeeping and refrain from leaving things at the common areas. For recalcitrant cases, the town council will enforce its by-laws and work closely with the fire authorities (Singapore Civil Defence Force) to resolve the obstruction problems. The town council should take into consideration the following when managing obstruction cases:

- **Be polite and courteous**: Respond to the resident politely and try to understand his or her concerns regarding the obstruction. Take note that the resident may be frustrated or upset with the obstruction which may have been going on for a long period of time.
- **Onsite assessment of the situation**: Conduct a site visit and meet up with the resident to better understand the obstruction problems. Assess the fire and safety hazards that the obstruction at the common property poses. Take photographs of the obstruction and advise

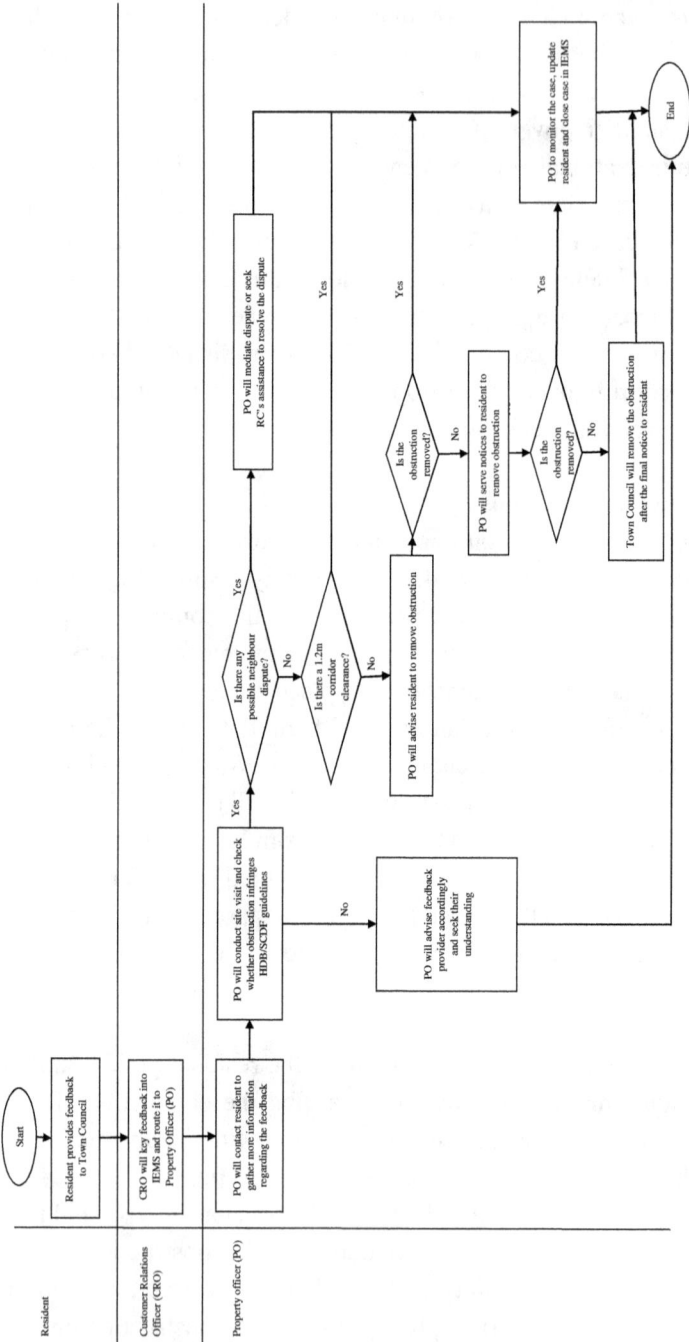

Figure 4.16   Flowchart for Obstruction Problems

the neighbours to remove any fire or safety hazard items, where applicable.

- **Monitor follow-up actions**: Monitor the follow-up actions taken to ensure that the neighbours have removed the obstruction according to the advice of the town council by a certain stipulated deadline. Keep the complainants informed on the follow-up actions and assure them that you are monitoring the situation closely.
- **Serve notices**: Serve a written warning to the residents who have failed to remove the obstruction by the stipulated deadline. Should the resident still refuse to comply, the town council may issue summons to enforce the removal of the obstruction. If the residents refuse to remove the obstruction, take appropriate measures to dispose of the obstruction using town council's contractor.
- **Monitor case closely**: Monitor the obstruction of common areas closely to prevent further reoccurrence. Encourage residents to keep the corridor and staircase landings obstruction-free and give feedback to the town council whenever there is obstruction.

(d) Neighbour dispute problems

Disputes between neighbours are usually difficult problems to resolve in the town council. There could be many contributing factors leading to the acrimonious relationships between or among neighbours (Figure 4.17). Issues relating to neighbour disputes include high-rise littering, noise nuisances, obstructions, racial or religious matters. Sometimes, the disputes have been ongoing for years, and residents are frustrated with one another as they cannot find any solution to the problems. The issues of the dispute may come under the jurisdiction of the town council or some other government agencies. Thus, it is important to identify the root causes of the disputes in order to find appropriate and sustained solutions. The town council should take into consideration the following when managing neighbour dispute cases:

- **Be responsive and attentive**: Respond quickly to the resident and listen attentively to his or her feedback or complaint about the neighbour. Try to understand his or her concerns and the dispute. Meet up with the resident onsite to understand the situation better, especially if

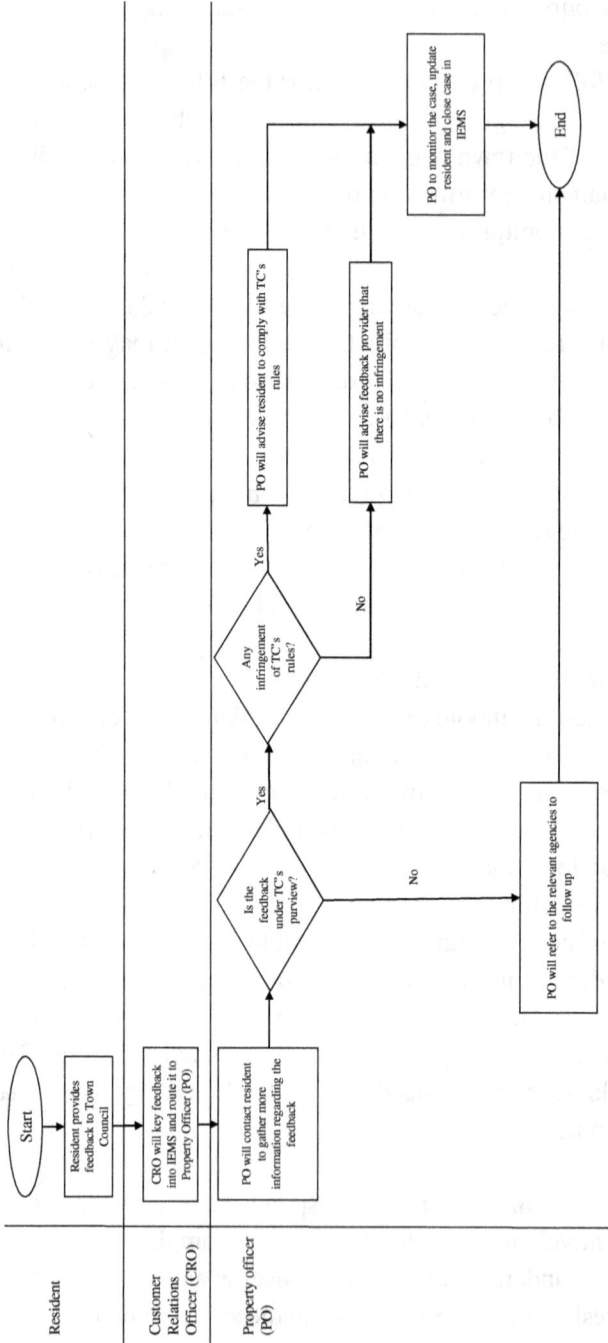

Figure 4.17 Flowchart for Neighbour Dispute Problems

the dispute is regarding anti-social acts, such as high-rise littering or obstruction. If possible, meet up with the neighbours separately to find out more about the dispute.

- **Communicate clearly**: Communicate clearly to the resident to assure the resident that you understand the issues and their concerns. Explain the follow-up actions to be taken to resolve the dispute. If necessary, advise the neighbours on the necessary actions to take to resolve the dispute.
- **Monitor progress closely**: Monitor the situation closely and check with the complainant on the progress of the situation. Conduct site visits to check on the situation and take photographs of any progress made.
- **Propose community mediation**: If the dispute continues, suggest community mediation to the disputing parties to find an amicable solution.
- **Monitor case closely**: Continue to monitor the dispute closely even after the mediation session has been or has not been conducted. For severe cases, the disputing parties may go to the courts for a settlement. Once the dispute is resolved, close the case in the IEMS and include the relevant for future reference.

(e) Animal/pet nuisance problems

Complaints regarding animal/pet nuisances are sensitive problems faced by the town council (Figure 4.18). It should be noted that the HDB has rules regarding the keeping of pets within HDB flats, while the town council generally does not permit the feeding of stray animals in housing estates. Over the years, there has been a growing number of animal lovers in the housing estates. Some would like to keep animals as pets within their flats while others advocate for the protection and welfare of animals. As such, the town council has to adopt a multi-pronged approach to manage animal and pet problems in the town. Very often, the town council will work closely with animal welfare groups to educate residents on responsible pet ownership, thus reducing the incidents of animal/pet nuisances. The town council should take into consideration the following when managing animal/pet nuisance cases:

- **Be sensitive and attentive**: Approach the complainant in a friendly and approachable manner and show empathy as he or she may be

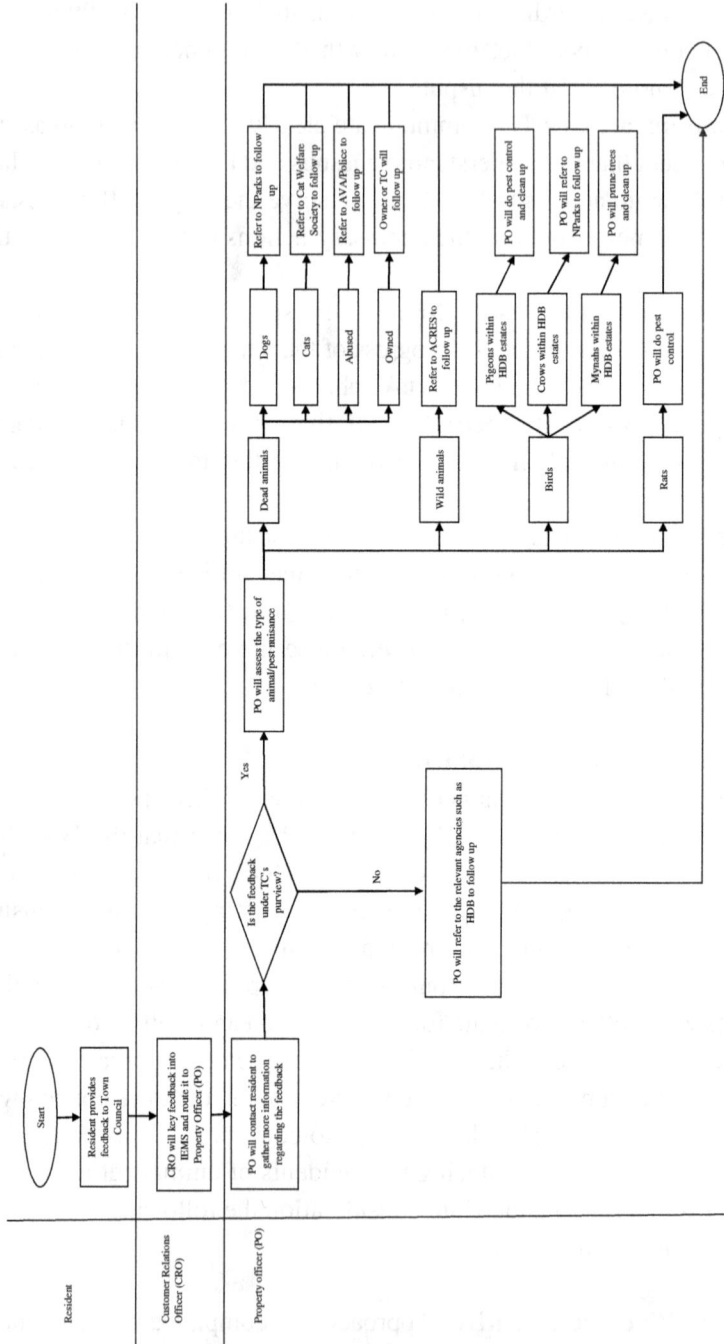

Figure 4.18   Flowchart for Animal/Pet Nuisance Problems

badly affected by the animal/pet nuisance. Some residents do not like animals and do not feel comfortable when there are animals in the housing estates. Certain racial groups are also sensitive to some animals. Thus, it is important for the town council to understand the sensitivity of handling animal/pet nuisance complaints.

- **Onsite inspection**: Conduct onsite inspections to better understand the animal/pet nuisance problems. Find out the cause of the nuisance so that appropriate follow-up actions can be taken to effectively resolve the problems. For instance, feeding of pigeons may attract more pigeons to the housing estate. Thus, educating the residents not to feed the pigeons and cleaning the housing estates more regularly may dissuage pigeons from coming to the area. Alternatively, it may also be necessary to cull the pigeons.

- **Referral to relevant agencies**: If the animal/pet nuisance is caused by animals outside the town council's jurisdiction, it may be necessary to refer such cases to the relevant government agencies for follow-up action. For instance, animals that are within the HDB flats should be dealt by the HDB, whereas issues relating to wild and stray animals are typically handled by NParks.

- **Monitor case closely**: Monitor the case closely to ensure that there is no reoccurrence of the nuisance in the town. If the problem persists, work with the relevant agencies to adopt various measures or take enforcement action.

(f) High-rise littering problems

Littering from residential flats has been a persistent public health issue (Figure 4.19). There have been several instances where residents have thrown litter from their high-rise flats, thus causing hygiene and safety problems. For example, lighted cigarette butts are a fire hazard and may cause damage to property. In relation to the more serious issue of high-rise killer litter, the town councils will work closely with the National Environment Agency (NEA) to conduct enforcement action to take enforcement action against any culprit who is caught engaging in such activities. Individuals who are found to have thrown high-rise killer litter will also be charged in courts to deter other would-be offenders. In relation to general high-rise littering cases, such as the throwing of tissues,

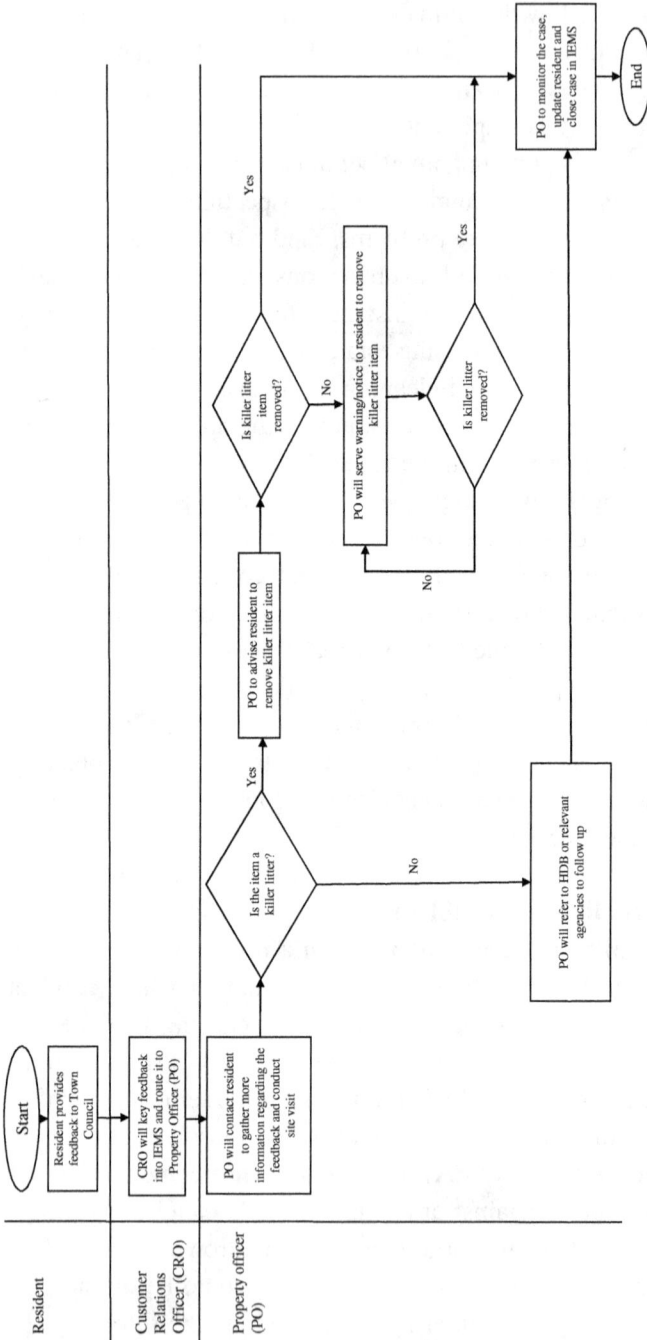

Figure 4.19   Flowchart for High-rise Littering Problems

cotton buds, sweet wrappers, food waste, or disposables, the town council will continue to educate both residents and the general public on the harms of high-rise littering and the importance of keeping Singapore clean. The town council should take into consideration the following when managing high-rise littering problems:

- **Be understanding**: When approaching the complainant, try to understand the high-rise littering problem and its impact on the resident's livelihood. The problem could be a long-standing recurring issue that has recurred numerous times. Check whether the high-rise litter is killer litter so that the town council can work closely with NEA to resolve the problem. Gather more information regarding the problem from neighbours, where possible.
- **Step up cleaning**: Deploy the conservancy contractor to step up the cleaning of the affected areas and monitor the situation closely. For killer litter cases, it may be necessary to cordon off the affected areas at the ground floor for safety purposes.
- **Communicate clearly**: Communicate to the complainant clearly the follow-up actions that will be undertaken to resolve the issue. For normal high-rise littering, put up educational posters and distribute notices to seek residents' cooperation in preventing high-rise littering.
- **Referral to relevant agency**: For high-rise killer litter, refer the case to NEA for enforcement action. If the high-rise litter problem persists, NEA will deploy surveillance camera to catch the culprit. Thereafter, NEA will prosecute the offender accordingly.
- **Monitor case closely**: Monitor the high-rise littering situation to ensure that the problem does not recur. Check with the complainant to confirm that the problem has been resolved.

(g) Mental health issues

Problems caused by mental health issues can often inconvenience and disrupt the lives of residents in a town (Figure 4.20). As the town council is not an expert in dealing with mental patients, the cases are usually referred to the mental health institutions or social service agencies for assistance. In some cases, the patients with mental health conditions can

Resident

Start

Resident provides feedback to Town Council

Customer Relations Officer (CRO)

CRO will key feedback into IEMS and route it to Property Officer (PO)

Property officer (PO)

PO will contact resident to gather more information regarding the feedback and conduct site visit

Is it a mental case?

Yes

No

PO to refer the case to relevant help agencies or IMH to follow up

PO will advise resident accordingly

PO to monitor the case, update resident and close case in IEMS

End

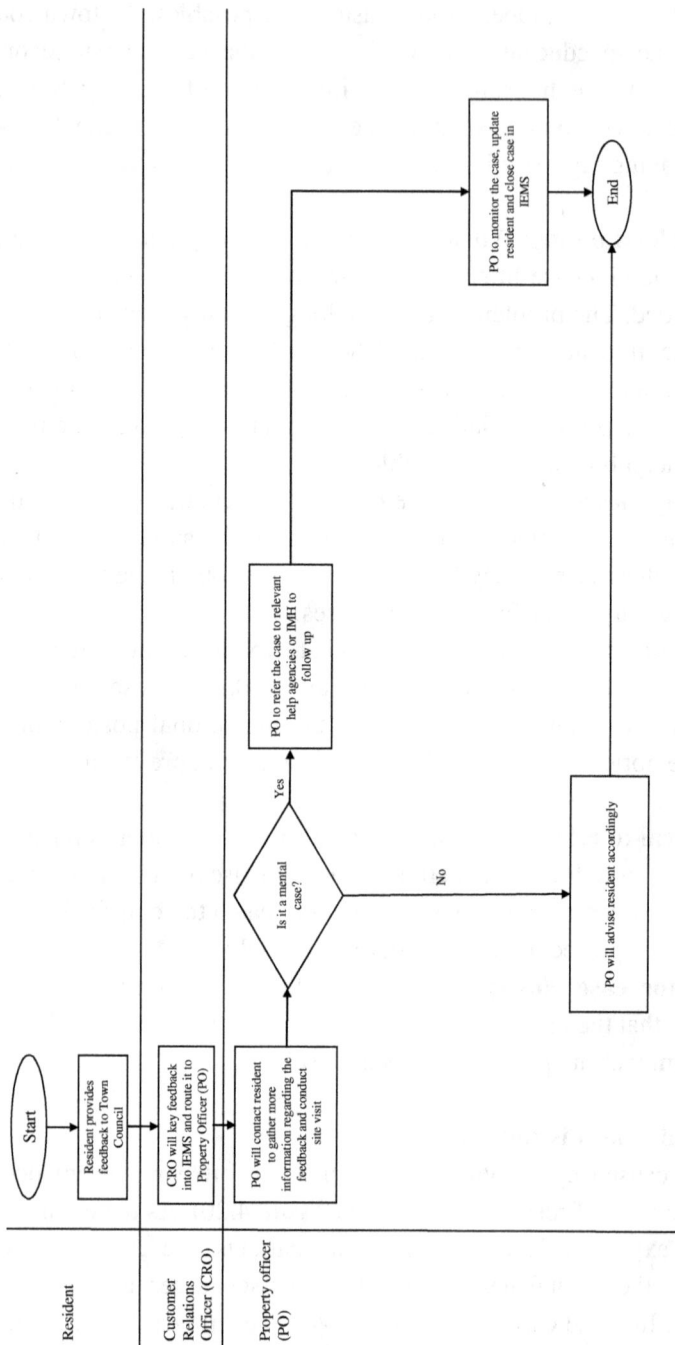

Figure 4.20   Flowchart for Mental Health Issues

be violent and thus pose safety risks to town council staff, workers and residents. In certain situations, the town council may choose to work with community partners and social service agencies to help the patients recover while minimising any disamenities caused to the community. The town council should take into consideration the following when managing mental health cases:

- **Be polite and courteous**: Be polite and courteous when approaching the complainant and find out details of the case. Conduct a site visit to understand the situation and the disamenities caused, such as littering problems, noise nuisance, vandalism, or loss of items.
- **Communicate clearly**: Communicate clearly to the complainant about the follow-up actions that will be taken to resolve the problems. If it is safe, talk to the patient with mental health conditions and his or her family members to understand their situation and discuss solutions to resolve the problems.
- **Seek help from agencies**: Seek help from mental health agencies and provide them with the relevant information to assist the patient with mental health conditions and his or her family members if necessary. Encourage the family members to send the patient for treatment as soon as possible. Refer them to social assistance agencies if they need financial support.
- **Monitor case closely**: Monitor the case closely to check whether the patient's well-being has improved or whether there has been any relapses.

4.11 Resident Engagement and Public Relations

Resident engagement and public relations are important responsibilities of the town council to build trust and confidence among residents with regard to the delivery of town council services. Based on the contact points with various stakeholders of the town, the town council must develop a customer relationship management plan. Through various engagement platforms such as formal meetings, informal meetings, residents' dialogues or town hall meetings, phones, social media or personal contacts, the town council will be able to identify the needs and aspirations of its stakeholders. This will enable the town council to formulate policies and implement maintenance programmes to provide a quality living environment for the residents and deliver quality services to fulfil the needs and aspirations of the residents.

With an effective customer service delivery system and well-trained staff, the town council will be able to build a strong rapport with its residents and stakeholders, and at the same time, deliver quality services. The IEMS provides a fully computerised and digitised platform to receive, respond and analyse feedback from residents and stakeholders so that prompt action can be taken to resolve problems. Each year, the 17 town councils in Singapore receive about 1 million feedback and complaints from residents and stakeholders. These feedback should be taken positively as opportunities for town councils to engage their residents and stakeholders, and improve on the quality of the services provided so as to satisfy the residents' needs. This will enhance the image of the town councils. It will also generate political mileage for the elected MPs.

As for public relations, the town council adopts a variety of strategies to publicise its activities, projects and plans. Every 5 years, the town council will prepare a master plan for the next 5 years after consulting the residents and various stakeholders. Very often, the master plan involves many ground-up initiatives which culminate towards a shared vision of all stakeholders of the town. The master plan will map out the strategic developments of the town, such as town improvement projects, estate upgrading programmes, enhancements to town council services, and initiatives to promote a sense of belonging and ownership among residents and stakeholders. The town council will organise a series of public relations activities to publish the master plan, hold exhibitions, organise town hall meetings and issue media releases.

Chapter 5

Cyclical Maintenance Management

5.1 Introduction

In the town council, cyclical maintenance works refer to works which must be routinely carried out based on the recommended life cycle of the building components and facilities or as directed by the Ministry of National Development. Cyclical maintenance works are necessary so as to ensure that the buildings and facilities are maintained in a good and serviceable condition. These works are scheduled in the yearly cyclical maintenance work programme and typically involve large sums of expenditure. As such, town councils will have to set aside funds from the monthly collection of service and conservancy charges into sinking funds for the cyclical maintenance expenditures.

Very often, the town councils will adopt a 10-year rolling plan for its cyclical maintenance works. The plan will typically highlight the various types of cyclical maintenance works and the estimated deadline for conducting such maintenance works in the respective financial year. This 10-year projection will assist the town councils to ensure that they have adequate sinking funds for the scheduled cyclical maintenance works. Figure 5.1 shows the steps involved in planning for the 10-year cyclical maintenance works rolling plan. To ensure that town councils set aside and have adequate funds for future cyclical maintenance works, the Ministry of National Development will require town councils to submit data relating to its cyclical maintenance works projections and the adequacy of its sinking funds, as and when required. This requirement is an

Property manager will update property data and last completed cyclical work items.

⬇

Project manager will confirm the dates of installation/last completion of cyclical work items.

⬇

Property manager to prepare a rolling 10-year projection of cyclical works due in each financial year.

⬇

Project manager will input the estimated cost of each cyclical work items in the 10-year projection.

⬇

Finance manager will check the availability of sinking funds for the 10-year projection.

⬇

General manager will approve the 10-year cyclical work plan and submit this to the town council chairman for approval.

⬇

The 10-year cyclical work plan will be presented to the town council for approval and thereafter implemented in each financial year.

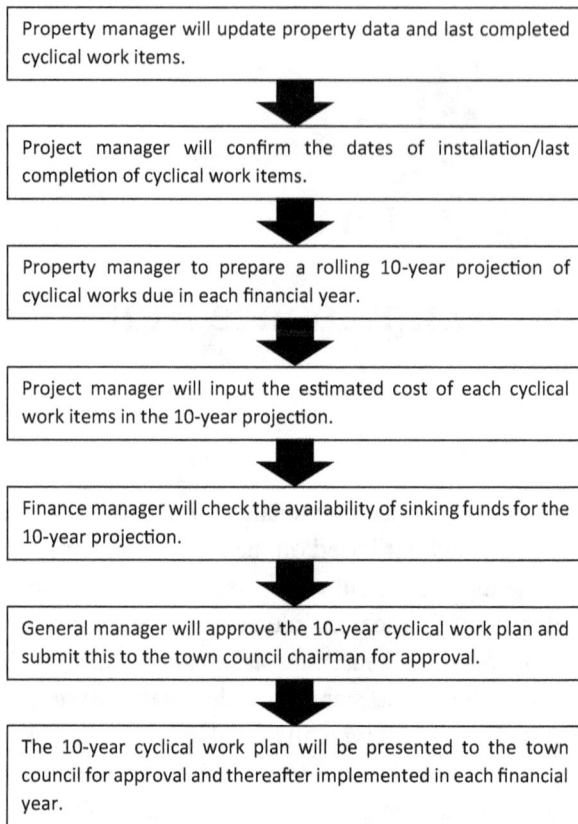

Figure 5.1   Planning of 10-year Cyclical Maintenance Work

integral component of the Town Council Management Report and helps to measure the financial health of the town councils.

While implementing the cyclical maintenance works, the town councils may decide to bring forward some works for a number of reasons. These include grouping of works or blocks to better capitalise on economies of scale, the fact that certain building components may no longer be in a serviceable condition, or due to HDB upgrading programmes. Such arrangements will also reduce inconvenience to residents. For example, the HDB neighbourhood renewal programme can be carried out together with repairs and redecorations of the blocks and minor improvement projects so that works can be carried out seamlessly at the same time.

5.2 Types of Cyclical Maintenance Work

To assist town councils in planning and executing cyclical maintenance, the ministry has provided a list of cyclical maintenance works and the recommended frequency of maintenance, as shown in Table 5.1.

Table 5.1   Types of Cyclical Maintenance Works and Recommended Life Cycles

S/No	Cyclical Maintenance Works	Cycle (years)
1	**Building**	
	• Repairs and redecoration	7
	• Replacement of metal features & claddings	28
	• Replacement of metal sun breaker	28
	• Replacement of metal roof	35
	• Replacement of connection system (metal roof, metal features & claddings and metal sun breaker)	14
	• Re-roofing of reinforced concrete roof	14
	• Replacement of clay-tiled roof	35
2	**Electrical system**	
	• Rewiring	25
	• Replacement of lamp post	20
	• Replacement of standby generator	25
3	**Water reticulation system**	
	• Replacement of water tank lining	10
	• Replacement of fibre-reinforced plastic water tank	20
	• Replacement of non-stainless steel water pipes	25
	• Replacement of booster pumps	7
	• Replacement of water pumps	12
	• Replacement of solenoid-operated pilot valve	12

(*Continued*)

Table 5.1   *(Continued)*

S/No	Cyclical Maintenance Works	Cycle (years)
4	**Lifts**	
	• Replacement of hoisting ropes/sheaves	7
	• Replacement of batteries of Automatic Rescue Device (ARD)	
	– Tabular/plante type	7
	– Maintenance-free type	5
	• Replacement of batteries for Emergency Battery Operated Power Supply (EBOPS)	
	– Plante type	7
	– Maintenance-free type	5
	• Total lift replacement	28
	• Replacement of lift position display panel	8
	• Replacement of lift inverter	6
5	**Escalator system**	
	• Replacement of step rollers, chain rollers	5
	• Replacement of step chain	7
	• Replacement of handrail and handrail rollers	7
	• Total replacement of escalator	30
6	**Fire-fighting and protection system**	
	• Replacement of fire pump control panel	15
	• Replacement of fire alarm panel	15
	• Replacement of fire pump	15
	• Replacement of pressure tank	5
	• Replacement of fire detector	5
7	**Waste management system**	
	• Replacement of individual Refuse Chute System (RCS) flushing system's control panel	12
	• Replacement of centralised RCS's refuse handling equipment	20
8	**Alarm alert system**	
	• Replacement of Alarm Alert System (AAS)	15

5.3 Annual Planning of Cyclical Maintenance Work

Every financial year, the town council will have to plan and set aside a budget for its cyclical maintenance works during the budget preparation period which is about 8 months (October/November) before the gazetting of the budget in June. According to Section 51(1) of the Town Councils Act, the town council shall prepare and display for public inspection the estimates of its revenue and expenditure for the next financial year not later than one month before the end of the financial year.

The property manager in charge of coordinating the cyclical maintenance works will collate the list of cyclical maintenance works due for the respective blocks and divisions (constituencies) based on the database and maintenance records of the blocks. The property manager will then provide an estimate to the finance manager of the budget required for the various types of cyclical maintenance work due for the financial year. The estimate shall be based on current tender prices or agreed cyclical maintenance fees for the respective types of works. For example, the estimated budget for the repairs and redecoration of a cluster of blocks shall be computed based on the scope of work for the Repairs and Redecorations (R&R), the current tender prices for similar R&R contracts and market trends of tender prices and inflation.

As for cyclical maintenance works relating to lifts, the property manager will liaise with the town council lift engineering team and respective lift firms to list out the cyclical work items due for replacement for the financial year. As lifts are specialist works with proprietary components, the cyclical works are carried out based on the work orders issued under its term contract with the agreed schedule of rates. For total replacement of lifts after the end of their lifespan (i.e. 28 years or earlier, depending on the serviceable conditions), an open tender is normally called.

The proposed list of cyclical maintenance works will be presented and discussed at the tender and contracts standing committee, which will in turn propose the budget for the town council's approval. Upon the town council's approval, the scheduled cyclical maintenance works will be procured during the financial year.

5.4 Procurement of Cyclical Maintenance Work

Once the town council has worked out the annual work plan for cyclical maintenance works, the respective property managers will liaise with their contract and project management teams to prepare for the tender of the scheduled cyclical maintenance works. The procurement process of cyclical maintenance works is shown in Figure 5.2. The contract and project management teams will gather the following information on the cyclical work items before submitting a call for tender:

- **Cyclical work items information**: Collate updated property data, such as blocks or work items due for cyclical maintenance, building plans and details of the last cyclical maintenance work done.

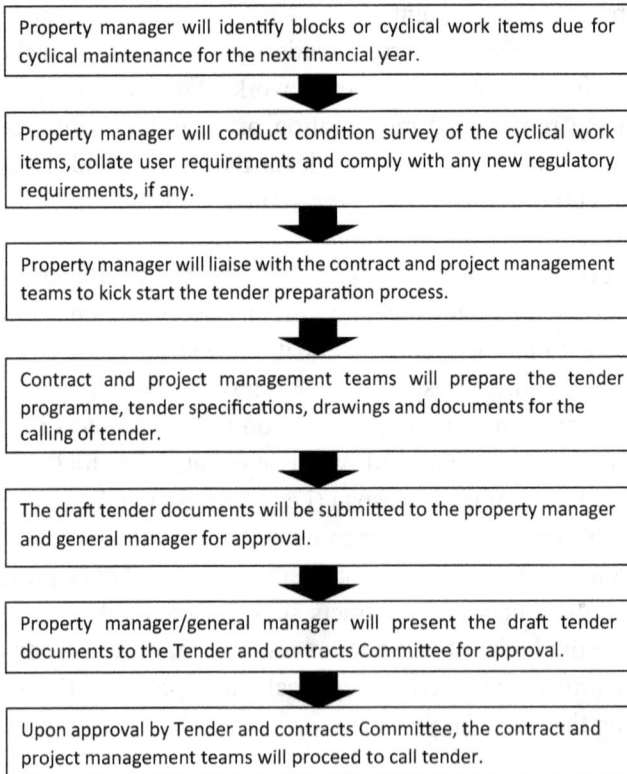

| Property manager will identify blocks or cyclical work items due for cyclical maintenance for the next financial year. |

| Property manager will conduct condition survey of the cyclical work items, collate user requirements and comply with any new regulatory requirements, if any. |

| Property manager will liaise with the contract and project management teams to kick start the tender preparation process. |

| Contract and project management teams will prepare the tender programme, tender specifications, drawings and documents for the calling of tender. |

| The draft tender documents will be submitted to the property manager and general manager for approval. |

| Property manager/general manager will present the draft tender documents to the Tender and contracts Committee for approval. |

| Upon approval by Tender and contracts Committee, the contract and project management teams will proceed to call tender. |

Figure 5.2   Procurement Process for Cyclical Maintenance Works

- **New regulatory requirements**: Identify any new regulatory requirements to that must be complied with in relation to the cyclical work items.
- **User requirements**: Identify user requirements based on complaints and suggestions from different stakeholders, such as MPs, residents, town councillors and community partners.
- **Condition survey report**: Conduct a condition survey of the cyclical work items, such as façade inspection of buildings and general surveys of the common property, mechanical equipment and electrical equipment.
- **Cost estimate**: Prepare a cost estimate of the cyclical work items for the council to approve the budget.
- **Tender documents**: Prepare tender specifications and documents for the calling of tender.

5.5 Tendering Process for Cyclical Maintenance Work

Each financial year, the town council will group the various types of cyclical maintenance works and submit calls for tender to select suitable contractors. As the contract sums for many cyclical maintenance works will normally exceed $70,000, the town council will be required to submit a call for open tender in accordance with the Town Councils Financial Rules. The town council will put up advertisements in the main newspapers to invite contractors to bid for the tenders. Tender briefings and site visits will be arranged, as and when necessary, so as to provide more information to tenderers for the projects.

Upon the submission of tender bids to the town council, the council will display the tender results on its noticeboard for public scrutiny. The contract and project management teams will proceed to evaluate the submitted tender bids. During the tender evaluation process, the bidders may be invited to attend tender evaluation interviews that are conducted by the town council. Once the tender evaluation is completed, the contract and project management teams will prepare the tender evaluation report and present it to the tender and contracts standing committee for approval. The tender and contracts standing committee will then make a recommendation as to the award of tender for the council to approve. The town council will then either approve or reject the award of tender at its meetings based on the majority of votes. Upon approval, the contract and project management teams will proceed to award the tender to the successful bidder and follow up with the signing of the contract.

According to the code of governance, the town council must ensure that the entire tender process is open, fair and transparent. The town council is publicly accountable to its residents and the general public for the utilisation of its funds. Therefore, it must exercise financial prudence and only enter into contracts that represent good value for money.

5.6   Tender Evaluation Method

As town councils are publicly accountable to their residents and the general public, they must exercise financial prudence and good corporate governance in the allocation of their funds and the award of contracts to their service providers. Based on the corporate governance principles of fair and open competition, the council must adopt a consistent approach when evaluating the tenders received, such that the town council can enter into contracts that represent good value for money. A common tender evaluation framework adopted by the town council in its tender evaluation process is the use of the Price Quality Method (PQM).

For the purposes of evaluating the tenders received, the relevant criteria would be both price and quality, with the weightage of each criteria being determined by the town council based on the type of work. For example, both price and quality are equally important (50% weightage split) in conservancy work contracts as the council will typically place greater emphasis on the quality of cleaning services in the town. However, contracts relating to playground equipment may instead have a 40% price and 60% quality weightage split as the quality of the design is of particular importance and performance of different proprietary playground equipment provided by different contractor may differ significantly.

Thus, the PQM tender evaluation framework will compute both the price and quality components of the submitted tender bids. The total PQM score is the sum of the price and quality scores respectively. The computation of the price and quality scores of a tender bid is illustrated as follows:

(a) **Price score** = Lowest tender price/Tenderer's price submitted × Price weightage,

(b) **Quality score** = Tenderer's total raw quality points/Highest total raw quality points × Quality weightage,

(c) **Total PQM score** = price score + quality score.

The quality attributes to be considered can include the following:

- **Financial records**: Bidders will submit their financial records to indicate their firms' assets, liabilities and cash flows. Reference can also be made to the financial ratings of the firms by independent agencies or financial institutions. The main purpose conducting this due diligence exercise is to ensure that the firm has adequate financial resources to complete the proposed project. The council will also check for any adverse financial and legal records, such as winding up proceedings, legal suits or suspensions or penalties imposed by the authorities.

- **Relevant track records (past and present performance)**: Bidders are required to submit information on their ongoing and past projects, including their performance records for completed projects. The council will also gather feedback on the past performance of completed projects from their respective clients or the relevant authorities, such as the Building and Construction Authority. The main purpose is to ensure that the successful bidder has the relevant experience and a good track record to complete the proposed project and achieve the project objectives relating to time, cost, safety and quality.

- **Organisation structure and proposed operations team**: Bidders will provide information on the setup of their firms and the key personnel involved in the proposed project, highlighting their qualifications and work experiences. This will include certified and accredited professionals required for the project, such as architects, engineers, project managers or facilities managers. The main purpose is to ensure that there is a competent team of professionals who can complete the project successfully.

- **Workplace health and safety records**: Bidders will need to declare any infringements of workplace health and safety rules, including warnings, suspensions, or fines imposed by authorities, such as the Ministry of Manpower or National Environment Agency. In addition, the bidders can provide any relevant workplace safety and health certifications to assure the council of their safety management systems.

- **Creative and innovation solutions (design, strategies or products)**: As part of their tender bid, bidders are to submit their creative designs and innovative solutions to the council for their consideration. These may include new or revolutionary design themes, plans, perspectives, concepts, or products that are to be implemented or used for the proposed project.

- **Commitment to sustainability**: Bidders will provide information on their environmental management systems, certifications (e.g. ISO standards) and achievements that are relevant to the proposed project.

- **Facilities management certifications**: Bidders may be required to submit facilities management certifications, such as accreditation from professional bodies or trade associations.

Chapter 6

Town Improvement Project Management

6.1 Town Council Plan

One of the objectives of setting up a town council is to provide more opportunities for residents of each town to take ownership of and participate in the improvement of the town. This will engender a greater sense of belonging among residents and various stakeholders of the town. Depending on the needs and aspirations of the residents, various town improvement projects can be implemented to enhance and upgrade the built environment. As required by the code of governance, every town council must have a structured and formalised Town Council Plan which will enable the town council to better plan, allocate and manage its funds and resources. The documented and approved Town Council Plan must ensure that the town council has adequate funds and resources to implement the plan. The plan includes both short-term programmes that can be implemented between 1 and 5 years and long-term programmes that go beyond 5 years.

In practice, many town councils will develop a Town Council Plan that spans across the parliamentary term of the elected MPs (usually between 3 and 5 years). The Town Council Plan should include planned estate maintenance and improvement or upgrading works relating to the residential, commercial, and common areas of the town. It should also include planned cyclical maintenance works, HDB upgrading programmes (i.e. neighbourhood renewal programmes, lift upgrading programmes, home improvement programmes and shop revitalisation schemes). The town council will also work out the estimated costs to implement the Town Council Plan in the estimated time frame that has agreed upon, taking into consideration the impact of ancillary factors like changes in the council's revenue, rising costs, new technologies and innovations.

In developing the Town Council Plan, the council will often engage its stakeholders through various platforms, such as the town council feedback system (Integrated Estate Management System or Lift Performance Management System), surveys, town hall meetings, dialogues, exhibitions and road shows. The purpose of these engagements is to better understand the needs and aspirations of the stakeholders and implement the plan in a manner that is in alignment with the expectations of all stakeholders and staff.

Once the Town Council Plan is developed, the town council will have to communicate the plan to all its stakeholders and set up a monitoring mechanism to ensure that the plan is successfully implemented. The council may use different channels and platforms such as notices, its websites, newsletters, social media, roadshows and media publicity to convey the plan and garner the support of its stakeholders. Very often, the town council will organise a publicity event to launch and exhibit the Town Council Plan for the next 5–10 years so that residents and stakeholders can understand the future development of the town. The exhibition can be held at the town centres or venues with high human traffic to ensure better outreach. It can also be a roving exhibition that moves around the different constituencies and divisions in the town.

After the launch of the Town Council Plan and exhibition, there could be further feedback and suggestions from various stakeholders and these can be used to refine the plan. In this way, the implementation of the Town Council Plan would have created opportunities for residents and stakeholders to contribute towards the management and improvement of the town.

6.2   Common Town Improvement Projects

Since the formation of town councils in Singapore, many towns have implemented different types of improvement projects to fulfil the needs and aspirations of their residents and stakeholders. At the same time, many towns have also evolved and developed their own unique character and identity. Based on the distinct vision of each town, each town council has worked tirelessly to improve their HDB housing estates in their own unique way and with a different emphasis as compared to other towns. For example, some town councils strive to build "Seamless Towns" to increase the connectivity and mobility in the towns. As a result, many covered linkways, drop-off porches and barrier-free access paths were built to connect blocks to transport nodes, such as bus-stops, pickup points, light rail stations and Mass Rapid Transit (MRT) stations. These improvement works have generally been well-received by residents, especially given Singapore's hot and humid climate and rainy monsoon seasons. The implementation of both horizontal and vertical barrier-free access amenities have also facilitated the mobility of residents, especially those residents who are wheelchair-bound or require the use of personal mobility devices to get around, including motorised scooters and motorised wheelchairs. In addition, the implementation of lift upgrading programmes has led to the building of new lifts or upgrading of existing lifts such that it now stops at every floor, which therefore provides convenient access for many residents to move from their flats to various places in the town.

To further support the improvement works in the towns, the Singapore government has implemented the Community Improvement Projects Committee (CIPC) funding scheme to provide subsidies for approved CIPC town improvement projects. The purpose of the CIPC fund is to encourage grassroots organisations (i.e. Citizens' Consultative Committees) to play a more proactive role in initiating town improvement projects that will benefit residents. Both the CCC and TC can apply for CIPC funding support for any improvement projects subject to the approval by the Ministry of National Development. CCC must then exercise prudence to ensure that the proposed projects will benefit the community and is good value for money when selecting the suitable service provider. Very often, open tender is called for improvement projects over S$70,000. Alternatively, the town council can also apply directly to the Ministry for CIPC funding. Table 6.1 provides a list of approved CIPC projects that will receive funding support from the government.

Table 6.1   Approved List of CIPC Projects

S/No	Types of Projects
1	**Basic facilities**
	• Staircases
	• Footpaths/pedestrian malls
	• Covered linkways
	• Drop-off points
	• Signages
	• Public toilets
2	**Recreational and leisure facilities**
	• Park shelters/shelters for facilities
	• Jogging/cycling tracks
	• Playground/courts
	• Residents' corners/senior citizens' corners
	• Community hall/community plaza
	• Seating facilities
	• BBQ pits
3	**Ancillary facilities**
	• Lift/lift lobby/lift landing
	• Closed-circuit television (CCTV)
	• Banner structure/noticeboards/letterboxes
	• Bicycle infrastructure
	• High contrast painted lines
	• Fans
4	**Innovative projects**
	• Projects that are innovative in promoting community bonding
5	**Special projects**
	• Projects that are urgent and needed for public safety and beneficial to the general public

6.3 Stakeholders' Engagement and Professional Consultations

As mentioned, every town council will formulate a Town Council Plan every 3–5 years to map out the planned maintenance, improvement and upgrading works in the town. Depending on the needs and aspirations of the residents and stakeholders, each town will have their own unique visions, missions and desired outcomes in respect of township management. It is therefore imperative for the town council to engage and receive feedback from their stakeholders through various sources. For example, the daily feedback received through the Integrated Estate Management System (IEMS) will highlight issues faced by residents. These include routine maintenance problems relating to conservancy and cleaning, building defects, mechanical and electrical failures, sanitary and drainage problems, horticulture and landscape works, pest control and hygiene issues, and social nuisance incidents. The feedback received will assist the town council to implement various measures to address the issues, and these can be performed together with routine maintenance or when carrying out cyclical maintenance works, such as repairs and redecorations works, replacement of mechanical and electrical parts or installation of new facilities.

Repairs and redecoration works are usually carried out once every 7 years depending on the condition of the blocks and common areas. It includes repainting works and minor repairs, such as the repairing of cracks, replacement of staircase railings, retiling of common areas or re-screeding of block aprons. As for other cyclical works such as lift parts replacement or upgrading, water tank replacement, reroofing and waterproofing, and replacement of mechanical and electrical installations, the council will consult the respective building professionals to obtain information on newer designs or innovative solutions suitable for the town council. These could include the installation of more energy-efficient water pumps or LED lighting.

Besides engaging the residents and building professionals, the town council will also engage its elected MPs, town councillors, grassroots and community partners when developing the Town Council Plan. Due to the profile of residents (age, race, education and income level or interests) and the location of different community organisations within the precincts and towns, the needs and aspirations of residents can differ to a large extent. Thus, the town council must adopt a more systematic and structured approach to identify the user requirements before implementing any improvement projects. This helps to ensure that user requirements are more comprehensively fulfilled and that any wastage is avoided (i.e. "white elephant" projects). The common approach is to conduct a survey and organise a residents' town hall meeting to discuss any proposed improvement projects. This will facilitate communication between the town council and the residents, thus improving consensus when implementing improvement projects. One common challenge faced by the elected MPs when visiting blocks or estates is that some residents are often "trigger happy" when making requests for improvement projects. However, residents sometime fail to understand that additional improvement projects will require more maintenance, thus increasing the cost of maintenance. In turn, this increased cost burden will add pressure on the town council to raise service and conservancy charges.

6.4　Understanding Users' Requirements

When implementing improvement projects for common property, it is important to understand the users' requirements so that suitable designs are adopted and appropriate equipment are installed. As improvement projects are carried out in different parts of the town and accessible to the general public, the council would have to take into consideration various issues, such as safety of the users and general public, ease of maintenance and any potential disamenity caused to nearby residents. Table 6.2 lists out the key considerations to identify users' requirements for some common improvement projects.

Table 6.2　Key Considerations to Identify Users' Requirements for Improvement Projects

S/No	Improvement Projects	Key Considerations
1	Covered linkway	• Simplicity and maintainability of design • Adequate cover for heavy rain and wind • Thermal insulation • Connecting points to blocks (safety & security concerns) • Bird proof design (bird nuisance concerns) • Anti-slip flooring materials • Proper gradient and drainage to keep floor dry
2	Drop-off porch	• Simplicity and maintainability of design • Adequate cover for heavy rain and wind • Bird proof design (bird nuisance concerns) • Anti-slip flooring materials • Proper gradient and drainage to keep floor dry
3	Fitness corner	• Age groups of users • Types of fitness equipment (cardiovascular and core muscles training)

Table 6.2   (*Continued*)

S/No	Improvement Projects	Key Considerations
		• Durable and robust equipment (indoor and outdoor equipment)
		• Location to avoid direct sunlight (sun orientation)
		• Seating facilities and social interaction nodes
4	Playground	• Age groups of children
		• Inclusiveness (special needs children)
		• Variety and replay value of equipment
		• Durability and maintainability of design
		• Location (sun orientation)
		• Proximity to pre-school premises
		• Seating facilities for caregivers
		• Safety standards for play equipment
		• Suitable flooring (preferably monolithic rubber flooring)
5	Community garden	• Champions and interest groups
		• Location suitable for planting (sun orientation)
		• Design and layout of planting plots (easy allocation to gardeners)
		• Community garden by-laws
		• Balloting of garden plots
		• Housekeeping rules
		• Skills training
		• Community sharing and bonding
6	Community hall	• Location and accessibility (causing nuisance to surrounding blocks)
		• Capacity of hall and types of functions/activities
		• Weatherproof, thermal insulation and ventilation
		• Water/electrical points and wash areas
		• Noise nuisance
		• Bird proofing measures
		• Ancillary areas for cooking
		• Anti-slip flooring for multiple purposes
		• Barrier-free access and railings
7	Multi-purpose hardcourt	• Location and accessibility
		• Location to avoid direct sunlight (especially morning sun affecting seniors' activities)

(*Continued*)

Table 6.2   (*Continued*)

S/No	Improvement Projects	Key Considerations
		• Anti-slip flooring
		• Adequate lighting for night events/activities
		• Flexibility to erect tentage for events
		• Barrier-free access and railings
		• Water/electrical points and wash areas
		• Elevated hardcourt with proper gradient
		• Hard wearing and robust floor finishings
8	Block directional signage	• Location (prominent and high user traffic)
		• Good contrast between signage background and letterings/graphics
		• Well-lighted with large font sizes/graphics
		• Watertight housing for lighted signages
		• Easy access for maintenance
		• Colour scheme for precinct and town identity

6.5 Town Identity and Branding

Since the introduction of the concept of town council management, many town councils have been developing their own character and identity in their respective towns. In order to nurture a stronger sense of belonging among residents and stakeholders, town councils will attempt to encourage more participation among stakeholders in their town identity and branding exercises. The common town identity markers and branding platforms include the following:

- **Landmark signage**: These landmark signages are built at precincts and gateways of towns so that residents and visitors can identify the precincts and towns.
- **Directional signage**: These directional signages (usually lighted) are installed at carpark entrances and block façades to guide drivers and users to the precincts and blocks in the towns. The colour scheme of the lighted directional signages can help to develop a identity for the precincts, divisions and towns.

- **Façade design and colour scheme**: Painting of murals and the use of colour schemes on the paintwork of block façades also help to create an identity for the blocks and precincts.
- **Landscape design**: Landscape designs and planting of trees also create a thematic living environment for residents and engenders a greater sense of belonging.
- **Standard design**: Standardising the design of improvement projects for precincts or divisions will also enhance identity, for example, adopting standard design and colour schemes for covered linkways, planting the same species of trees and shrubs within precincts or towns, or using the same colour scheme for directional and block signages.
- **Banner post design**: Unique banner post designs for each precinct or residents' committee zone may also help to create a common identity among residents.
- **Precinct naming**: Precinct landmarks and names can also create a sense of belonging among residents staying in the same precinct.
- **Thematic vision of town**: Town councils can adopt different themes to brand their towns, such as the themes of a "liveable town", "green town", "family-friendly town", "inclusive town", or "senior-friendly town".

Besides the installation of town identity markers within the town, the town council can also adopt various modes of communication to brand its town. These include the launching of the Town Council Plan and organising exhibitions within the town, publicity through the media and new media channels, displaying the town council's messages through billboards, banners and noticeboards, conveying information through town council's newsletters, flyers and websites. Some town councils may even organise a welcome party for new residents and a town day for residents to celebrate their achievements in managing the towns. Every town council is also required by the Town Councils Act to publish an annual report and prepare its audited statement to be submitted to Parliament through the Ministry of National Development.

Chapter 7

Town Upgrading Programmes

7.1 Introduction

As a town matures, it is an unavoidable fact that the buildings and amenities will deteriorate, the residents will age and their children will grow up. Consequently, the needs and aspirations of residents is in constant flux and remains ever-changing. Furthermore, new residents may move into the towns due to various reasons, such as resettlement, resale of housing units in the open market, new public housing flats built (Housing and Development Board's Build-To-Order [BTO] flats) or newborn babies. It is also common for residents who have stayed in the same town for many years to begin developing a sense of familiarity with the living environment there and to form meaningful bonds with their neighbours and friends in the community.

To facilitate graceful ageing in the community and enable residents to age in place, the Singapore government has been continuously revitalising and upgrading HDB estates since the 1990s. These upgrading programmes help to rejuvenate older estates both within and outside the individual HDB flats so as to keep the town functional and the community intact. Over the years, various types of upgrading programmes have been implemented to benefit thousands of residents staying in public housing estates.

Besides the upgrading of public housing flats, the government has also implemented an Estate Upgrading Programme (EUP) for residents living in private housing to also enjoy upgrades to the living environment outside their homes.

Over the years, the HDB and town councils have worked closely to implement the various town upgrading programmes. The upgrading programmes have also evolved to meet the changing needs and aspirations of the residents. The key estate upgrading programmes are listed as follows:

(a) **Main Upgrading Programme (MUP) (1990–2007)**: The MUP was introduced in 1990 to upgrade older estates at the precinct, block and flat levels. The scope of work included the upgrading of toilets within the flats, addition of floor space (space adding item), and addition of amenities such as covered linkways, drop-off car porches, fitness corners, playgrounds, and multi-purpose courtyards. As the upgrading works were carried out while residents continued to stay in their homes, extra care was taken to ensure that residents' remained safe and comfortable during the implementation of these measures and the conduct of construction work.

(b) **Interim Upgrading Programme (IUP) (1993–2001)**: The IUP was introduced in 1993 to upgrade older estates built in the 1980s. The improvement works included block and precinct upgrades, including façade treatments, void deck tiling or resurfacing, landscaping works and the installation of other amenities within the precinct (i.e. covered linkways, precinct landmarks, directional signs and gardens).

(c) **Lift Upgrading Programme (LUP) (Since 2001)**: The LUP was introduced in 2001 with the aim of upgrading existing HDB blocks to provide direct access to all units where technically feasible. Blocks which were successfully upgraded would have lifts that could stop at every floor, providing barrier-free access to residents and allowing seniors to age in place. As each HDB block has its own unique design, several different approaches had to be implemented to facilitate the upgrading works (i.e. by either creating new lift door openings in an existing lift shaft or by installing a new external lift shaft that is connected to each floor of the HDB). As part of the LUP, the lift landing areas were also upgraded, including re-screeding and re-tiling works or even the installation of lift surveillance systems (i.e. closed-circuit television cameras) within the lift cage.

(d) **Home Improvement Programme (HIP) (Since 2007)**: The HIP was introduced in 2007 with the aim of upgrading the interior of HDB flats. The scope of work included the installation of new clothes hanging poles, water-proofing and upgrading existing toilets, spalling concrete repairs, and the replacement of main doors and gates. As the work was carried out while the residents continued to stay in their flats, appropriate measures were taken to ensure the safety and comfort of residents.

(e) **Neighbourhood Renewal Programme (NRP) (Since 2007)**: The NRP was introduced in 2007 to upgrade the precincts and blocks within the estates. Precincts and blocks built before 1995 and not previously upgraded under MUP/IUP are eligible for this upgrading programme. As part of the NRP, there has been active engagement with residents to understand their needs and identify suitable improvements to their living environments. Surveys and townhall meetings have also been conducted to gather feedback and suggestions to improve the neighbourhood. Improvement projects include the creation of covered linkways, drop-off porches, community gardens, landscaping, multi-purpose courtyards, community halls, fitness corners and playgrounds.

(f) **Enhancement for Active Seniors (EASE) (Since 2012)**: The EASE was introduced in 2012 to provide features which will enhance the safety and comfort of seniors living in HDB flats. These include the provision of slip-resistant treatment to the toilet floor within the HDB, installation of grab bars within the flat (and in the toilet), and ramps within the flat to improve accessibility.

(g) **Selective En Bloc Redevelopment Scheme (SERS) (Since 1995)**: The SERS was introduced in 1995 to redevelop older blocks so as to optimise land use. Affected residents were given appropriate compensation based on the market valuation and assured allocation of a new flat at the designated replacement site at subsidised prices.

(h) **Revitalisation of Shops Scheme (ROS) (Since 2007)**: The ROS was introduced in 2007 to enhance the vibrancy and competitiveness of HDB shops so as to better serve the needs of residents. The ROS scheme comprises the following components: (i) co-funding for upgrading of common area, (ii) co-funding for optional shopfront improvement works, (iii) co-funding for promotional events, (iv) rent-free periods for tenants to renovate their shops, and (v) start-up fund for the formation of Merchants' Association.

(i) **Estate Upgrading Programme (EUP) (Since 2000)**: The EUP was introduced in 2000 to upgrade the ageing infrastructure of private housing estates. This scheme is fully funded by the government and includes upgrading works to the external areas of private estates, such as footpaths, lighting, drainage, barrier-free access, estate markers, park furniture, playground equipment, landscaping works and communal facilities.

(j) **Lift Enhancement Programme (LEP)**: The LEP was introduced in 2018 to upgrade the older lifts to be on par with the newer lifts. Under the LEP, HDB will fund about 90% of the town council's costs to install the recommended enhancement features. Lifts that are not yet equipped with some or all of the enhancement features and have been in operation for 18 years or less (as of 2018) would be eligible for the LEP.

7.2 Key Estate Upgrading Programmes

(a) Neighbourhood Renewal Programme (NRP)

The HDB NRP is carried out by the town councils and is fully funded by the government (about S$4,700 per dwelling unit since 2014). Its main purpose is to upgrade and improve the amenities in two or more contiguous precincts in a neighbourhood. Very often, the number of blocks selected for the NRP is about 10–30 blocks (1,000–3,000 dwelling units). This allows the town council to leverage on economies of scale and also gives them more flexibility when upgrading the precincts and installing additional amenities. Given the scale of the upgrading works, the town council can also coordinate the upgrades such that the precinct or neighbourhood can have a unique feeling, and inculcate a sense of belonging among residents, shop owners and tenants. The scope of work for NRP entails both block and precinct improvements. The list of approved improvement work items for NRP is listed in Table 7.1.

The key objectives of the NRP are as follows:

- Upgrade the quality of older HDB estates and bring them closer to the standards of the newer HDB estates.
- Keep the communities intact and enable residents to age in place.
- Enhance the value of the older HDB flats and shops.

Table 7.1 List of Approved Improvement Work Items for NRP

S/No	Improvement Work Items
1	**Block level**
	• Residents' corner
	• Lift lobby tiling and re-screeding
	• Lift lobby lighting
	• Lighting
	• Study corner
	• New letterboxes
	• Block signage
	• Corridor tiling and re-screeding
	• Corridor lighting
	• Lift surveillance system
	• Seating area at void decks
	• Bicycle station
2	**Precinct level**
	• Covered linkway
	• Canopy to blocks
	• Recreational mall
	• Hardcourt/badminton court
	• Playground
	• Outdoor seating area
	• Pavilion/shelter
	• Pergola/trellis
	• Pebble walk/foot reflexology path
	• Landscaping
	• Drop-off point/porch
	• Fitness corner/station
	• Bird handing/singing area
	• Perimeter enhancement/precinct markers
	• Landmark structure
	• Driveway
	• Multi-purpose court/basketball court
	• Footpath/pavement/jogging track
	• Amphitheatre
	• Paved area/activity plaza
	• Street soccer pitch
	• Community gardening area

- Engage residents and shop owners/tenants in shaping their living and operating environment.
- Enable town councils to carry out block and precinct improvement works in a neighbourhood.

The NRP process kicks off when the Ministry of National Development invites the town councils to nominate eligible blocks, precincts or neighbourhoods for the programme. Upon the receipt of an invitation to nominate blocks for NRP, the town councils will consult their elected Members of Parliament (MPs), town councillors, community leaders, residents and staff to identify the blocks for nomination. Key considerations in selecting the blocks and precincts include the age of the blocks, conditions of the amenities in the precincts and neighbourhoods, and the needs and aspirations of the residents and shop owners/tenants. Every town council will then submit a list of blocks and precincts eligible for the NRP to the ministry. The nominated precincts will then be ranked in order of priority by the town councils.

Once the ministry has approved the nominated precinct or precincts submitted by town councils for the NRP, the town council will proceed to form NRP working committees for the selected precinct or precincts. A typical NRP working committee shall comprise representatives from the town council, HDB, grassroots organisations, and consultants. The entire NRP process as shown in Figure 7.1 will take about 36 months from the date of announcement to the completion of work. The working committee will work with the project consultants throughout the design development process to the consensus-gathering stage. To ensure that the NRP will benefit the majority of residents of the selected precinct or precincts, at least 75% of the eligible flat owners must indicate their support for the proposed design and programme. As part of the consensus-gathering exercise, the working committee will normally conduct a survey to allow residents to choose the types of improvement work items from the approved list as provided by HDB, as shown in Table 7.1. An example of the results of the NRP consensus-gathering survey results is shown in Figure 7.2.

The consensus-gathering survey and town hall meetings with residents and stakeholders will provide useful information for the working committee to understand the needs and aspirations of the residents and stakeholders for the blocks and precincts. During the design stage, the

```
                    ┌─────────────────────────────┐
          ┌─────────│     Announcement of NRP     │
          │         └─────────────┬───────────────┘
          │                       ▼
          │         ┌─────────────────────────────┐
          │         │   Form NRP working committee │
          │         └─────────────┬───────────────┘
          │                       ▼
          │         ┌─────────────────────────────┐
          │         │     Design development      │◄────────┐
          │         └─────────────┬───────────────┘         │   ┌──────────────────────┐
          │                       ▼                         │   │  Residents' feedback  │
┌──────────────┐   ┌─────────────────────────────┐         │   └──────────────────────┘
│  12 months   │   │     Public consultation     │─────────┘
└──────────────┘   └─────────────┬───────────────┘
          │                       ▼
          │         ┌─────────────────────────────┐
          │         │      Design refinement      │
          │         └─────────────┬───────────────┘
          │                       ▼
          │         ┌─────────────────────────────┐
          │         │     Consensus gathering     │
          │         └─────────────┬───────────────┘
          │                       ▼
          │         ┌─────────────────────────────┐
          └─────────│           Tender            │
          ┌─────────└─────────────┬───────────────┘
┌──────────────┐                  ▼
│  18 to 24    │   ┌─────────────────────────────┐
│   months     │   │        Construction         │
└──────────────┘   └─────────────┬───────────────┘
          │                       ▼
          │         ┌─────────────────────────────┐
          └─────────│         Completion          │
                    └─────────────┬───────────────┘
                                  ▼
                    ┌─────────────────────────────┐
                    │   Handover to Town Council   │
                    └─────────────────────────────┘
```

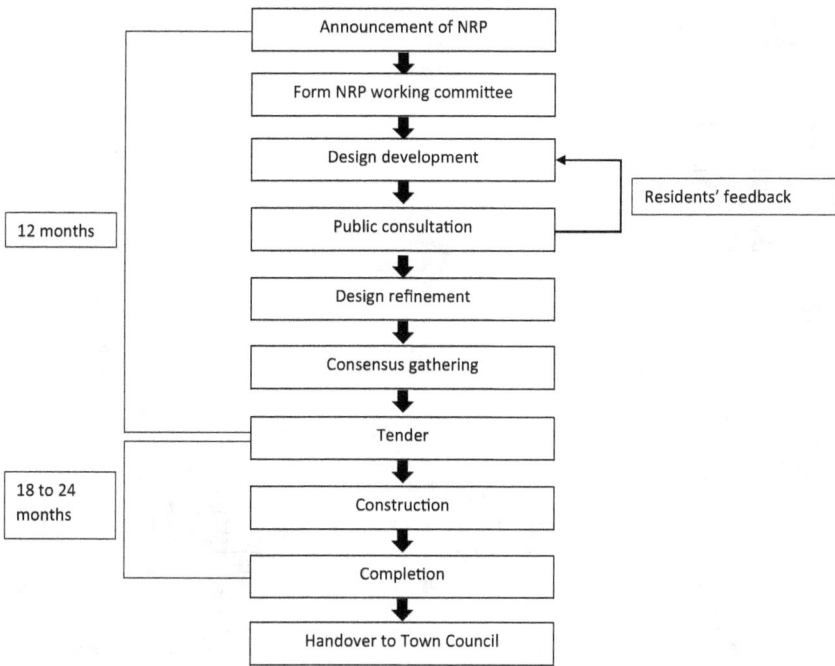

Figure 7.1 Flow Chart of NRP Process

working committee will work closely with the project consultants to ensure that the proposed design will obtain at least 75% support from the residents. Once the proposed design is ready, the working committee will organise an exhibition to share the proposed design with the residents and stakeholders. A poll is then conducted to determine if at least 75% of flat owners are in support of the NRP. Once the mandate is obtained, the town council will seek HDB's approval as landlord to implement the upgrading programme. Upon HDB's approval has been obtained, the town council will call an open tender to select a suitable contractor for the NRP project. The appointed contractor will then proceed with the upgrading works until the works have been completed. Thereafter, the project will be handed over to the town council for future maintenance.

(b) Lift Upgrading Programme (LUP)
The LUP was first implemented in 2001 to provide residents with direct lift access (barrier-free access) to their flats. About 5,300 HDB blocks

NEIGHBOURHOOD RENEWAL PROGRAMME (NRP)
邻区更新计划

	List of Improvement Items 改进的项目	Blocks												
1	(2) Lift Surveillance System （电梯监控系统）	40	59	45	63	40	33	52	36	32	22	55	5	482
2	(15) Drop-off porch / Point （乘客上下车亭）	28	51	37	69	31	32	46	26	19	35	32	3	409
3	(5) Covered linkway （有盖走廊）	19	43	46	30	30	47	63	26	18	16	44	5	387
4	(16) Fitness corner （健身角落）	39	50	30	72	21	18	33	25	25	21	23	4	361
5	(6) Canopy to blocks （雨蓬）	12	38	36	17	35	30	40	18	19	17	37	4	303
6	(21) Footpath / Pavement / Jogging track （行人走道 / 跑道）	29	25	28	18	23	27	34	16	24	23	31	6	284
7	(7) Recreational mall （休闲广场）	18	25	30	24	20	10	27	22	22	17	26	6	247
8	(4) Seating area at void decks （组屋底层休闲处）	18	20	24	21	20	10	36	23	28	10	19	3	232
9	(14) Landscaping （景观 / 园艺）	17	24	15	26	23	16	18	20	15	21	29	3	227
10	(20) Multi-purpose court / Basketball court （多用途场所）	22	18	27	36	15	12	15	19	16	17	19	5	221
11	(24) Study corner （阅读角落）	26	19	19	16	16	8	31	17	31	14	20	2	219
12	(25) Community gardening area （社区花园）	17	25	13	45	15	9	15	11	20	10	18	1	199
13	(10) Outdoor seating area （户外休息处）	15	21	12	15	17	12	21	22	17	11	25	3	191
14	(26) Residents' corner （居民休闲角落）	9	28	8	50	9	9	17	9	17	14	16		186
15	(13) Pebble walk / Foot reflexology path （足底按摩走道）	12	14	22	12	14	15	18	13	19	15	27	2	183
16	(9) Playground （儿童游乐场）	21	17	22	15	13	9	15	11	17	11	14	1	166
17	(11) Pavilion / Shelter （亭子）	20	12	18	11	16	12	29	15	8	7	15	2	165
18	(32) Corridor tiling & Rescreeding （更换走廊洋灰地板或地砖）	10	9	13	27	17	15	11	7	16	11	20	5	161
19	(31) Lighting （电灯）	15	17	10	5	10	11	17	11	21	16	18	2	153
20	(1) New letterbox （更换信箱）	9	16	9	6	14	8	18	8	24	7	15	5	139
21	(8) Hardcourt / Badminton court （广场 / 羽球场）	14	16	13	13	11	11	18	12	7	7	9	2	133
22	(3) Block directional signage （组屋指示牌）	9	21	10	11	11	8	15	12	11	8	12	3	131
23	(23) Paved area / Activity plaza （活动广场）	6	7	15	8	11	7	19	7	17	11	11	7	126
24	(22) Amphitheatre （露天剧场）	17	8	10	3	7	8	10	12	9	9	13	1	107
25	(30) Lift lobby lighting （更换电梯大厅电灯）	8	10	16	3	5	3	18	5	14	8	12	2	104
26	(28) Bicycle station （脚车停放处）	10	12	5	6	18	8	12	2	10	4	6	1	94
27	(27) Street soccer pitch （街头足球场）	8	5	7	9	8	8	13	15	7	4	5	2	91
28	(29) Lift lobby tiling & Rescreeding （更换电梯大厅地砖）	4	6	7	6	5	3	14	9	5	6	8	2	75
29	(12) Pergola / Trellis （凉棚）	8	7	5	5	8	4	9	4	9	4	8		71
30	(19) Landmark structure （地标建筑）	5	5	2	2	3	6	9	6	6	7	10	3	64
31	(18) Perimeter enhancement / precinct markers （邻里地标）	4	8	3		5	3	8	6	8	9	6		60
32	(17) Bird-hanging area （观鸟台）	3	2	5	4	4	3	8	2	4	4	1		40
	Number of Household per Block	84	116	110	118	96	76	110	80	88	68	99	14	1059
	Number of Household per Block responded	69	100	88	96	77	61	90	68	78	57	87	12	883
	% of Household per block responded	82.14	86.21	80.00	81.36	80.21	80.26	81.82	85.00	88.64	83.82	87.88	85.71	83.38

Figure 7.2   Survey Results of Consensus Gathering for NRP

which were built in the early years do not have lifts that stop at every floor to provide barrier-free access to every flat. Due to the changing needs of residents and an ageing population, the government has introduced a co-sharing funding scheme to expedite the LUP. With the government's sub-sidy and town council's co-sharing of the cost, flat owners only need to pay up to a maximum of S$3,000 (about 5–15% of the cost) for the LUP. The actual cost of the lift upgrading works will depend on the block design and configurations. Existing lifts can be upgraded to provide access to every floor or new lift shafts can be added to provide direct access to certain segments of the blocks. A new lift landing will be provided for every floor after upgrading. Over the years, the LUP has undergone various improvements and innovations, such as the installation of machine-roomless lifts, bubble (shaftless) lifts, smaller lifts (home lifts for low-rise flats) and reconfiguration of lift access with new entry points to residents' flats.

The LUP will only be implemented if 75% or more of the eligible Singapore citizen flat owners in the block without direct lift access vote for the programme. A poll will be conducted once the proposed design of the upgraded lift is conveyed to the flat owners. As the LUP is carried out by the town council, the council may organise an exhibition to display the lift upgrading proposal so as to secure the required 75% votes. The town council may face certain resistance from some residents when attempting to garner support for the LUP. Typically, such objections are based on the following reasons:

- Residents staying at the lower floors (second or third storey) feel that they do not need the lift to stop at every floor.
- Residents who plan to move out of their existing flats refuse to co-share the LUP cost.
- Residents prefer to walk up one or two flights of stairs to their flats even though the existing lifts do not stop at their floors.
- Residents do not want to experience the disamenity caused during the upgrading work.
- Different groups of lobbyists are against the LUP due to the different subsidies given by the government (subsidy is tiered according to flat type and citizenship).

Thus, the working committee has to work closely with community leaders and residents to help them understand the short-term inconveniences and long-term benefits of LUP. In high-rise living, vertical transportation and barrier-free access have significant impact on the quality of life of residents. This is especially so for an ageing community with many seniors gradually losing their mobility. However, some residents may find it difficult to empathise with individuals who require direct lift access as they themselves have not suffered any loss of mobility (due to age, illness or the occurence of accidents).

The LUP process is similar to the NRP as the ministry will initiate the programme by inviting town councils to select and prioritise eligible blocks for lift upgrading. Town councils will then nominate the blocks based on the age of the lifts, performance of the lifts, feedback from residents, design of the blocks, technical viability and estimated cost of lift upgrading. The entire lift upgrading process will usually take between 12 and 36 months to complete depending on the proposed design and number of blocks undergoing the programme. The key stages of LUP are shown in Figure 7.3.

Since the implementation of the LUP, more than 5,000 HDB blocks have had their lifts upgraded to provide direct access to every floor. This has brought about immense benefits to the residents and their visitors, especially those with mobility and accessibility challenges, such as seniors, wheel-chair users, people with special needs, young children,

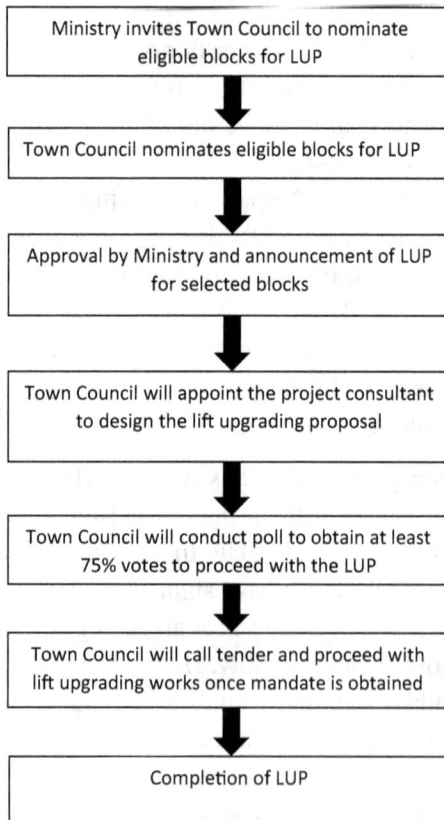

```
┌─────────────────────────────────────────┐
│   Ministry invites Town Council to nominate │
│        eligible blocks for LUP            │
└─────────────────────────────────────────┘
                    ↓
┌─────────────────────────────────────────┐
│ Town Council nominates eligible blocks for LUP │
└─────────────────────────────────────────┘
                    ↓
┌─────────────────────────────────────────┐
│   Approval by Ministry and announcement of LUP │
│           for selected blocks             │
└─────────────────────────────────────────┘
                    ↓
┌─────────────────────────────────────────┐
│ Town Council will appoint the project consultant │
│     to design the lift upgrading proposal │
└─────────────────────────────────────────┘
                    ↓
┌─────────────────────────────────────────┐
│ Town Council will conduct poll to obtain at least │
│      75% votes to proceed with the LUP    │
└─────────────────────────────────────────┘
                    ↓
┌─────────────────────────────────────────┐
│ Town Council will call tender and proceed with │
│ lift upgrading works once mandate is obtained │
└─────────────────────────────────────────┘
                    ↓
┌─────────────────────────────────────────┐
│           Completion of LUP               │
└─────────────────────────────────────────┘
```

Figure 7.3   Flow Chart for Lift Upgrading Programme (LUP)

pregnant women, movers, delivery riders, contractors and individuals suffering from sickness.

As of January 2022, only about 140 HDB blocks have not undergone the LUP. This was due to a number of reasons, including the unique block designs, site constraints or the prohibitive cost of implementing the upgrades. For these blocks, the government has provided a lift access housing grant (up to S$30,000) for residents with urgent need of direct access due to medical conditions or for mobility reasons. Eligible residents under the HDB Lift Access Housing Grant (LHG) can buy a new or existing flat that has direct lift access.

(c) Home Improvement Programme (HIP)

The HIP was implemented in 2007 to help flat owners upgrade their ageing flats and provide barrier-free access within the flat. The key objectives are to resolve maintenance problems, such as spalling concrete, water leakages between floors, waste pipe failures, and upgrading of electrical load. The HIP comprises three key components: essential, optional and EASE improvement works.

The essential improvement works are compulsory and include the following:

- repair spalling concrete/structural cracks;
- replace waste/soil discharge stacks;
- replace pipe sockets with new clothes drying rack (senior-friendly design); and
- upgrade electrical load.

The optional improvement works will be chosen by the flat owners and include the following:

- package to upgrade existing toilet(s)/bathroom(s) including waterproofing;
- new entrance door;
- new entrance grille gate; and
- new refuse chute hopper.

The EASE improvement works are optional and include the following:

- slip-resistant treatment to floors of toilets/bathrooms;
- grab bars in toilets and bathrooms; and

- ramps to navigate level differences within the flat and at the main door entrance.

The HIP process is also initiated by the invitation of the ministry to nominate blocks eligible for the programme. The town council will work closely with its elected MPs or advisers of the grassroots organisations to nominate suitable blocks for HIP. Very often, about 8–10 blocks will be packaged together for the HIP to enjoy better economies of scale for the upgrading works. The government fully funds the essential improvement works and provides subsidies for a major portion of the optional improvement works. The subsidy ranges from 87.5% to 95% depending on the flat type. The duration of the HIP is about 18–24 months. Each flat will take about 10 working days to complete its HIP.

Once the blocks for HIP were approved by the ministry, the town council will convey the message to the residents through notices, town hall meetings and announcements by the elected MP or grassroots adviser. A working committee for the HIP is then formed comprising the elected MP or grassroots adviser, representatives from the grassroots organisations, HDB and town council. HDB will take the lead and work closely with the working committee to implement the HIP. The HIP contractor will be appointed by HDB and will come up with various proposals for the HIP improvement work items. When the HIP proposals are ready, the working committee and HDB will organise an exhibition and polling exercise for residents to vote for the essential improvement works and choose the optional improvement work items. Once at least 75% of the eligible Singapore citizen flat owners have voted in favour of the essential improvement works, the working committee can proceed with the programme.

As the profile and needs of residents are different, it is important for the working committee to conduct a pre-survey to better understand the support level and preferences of the residents. Special attention must be paid to the design of the toilet/bathroom upgrading package, such as tiling, sanitary fittings, and designs. The residents will be given a few design options (usually three proposed designs) to choose for both essential and optional improvement work items. The provision of design options will improve the support level for the upgrading programme.

The HIP has benefitted many flat owners in upgrading their flats. They enjoy cost savings due to the economies of scale of upgrading many flats concurrently and enhancing the living environment of many residents at the same time.

(d) Revitalisation of Shops Scheme (ROS)

The ROS was introduced in 2007 to boost the vibrancy and competitiveness of HDB retail shops in town centres and neighbourhood centres. As towns develop, more new amenities will be added. These include commercial shopping centres and other municipal shops. The needs and shopping habits of residents may also change with the times. For instance, the outbreak of COVID-19 has expedited online shopping and e-commerce. Many residents including seniors have learnt to purchase food, groceries and do their shopping online. These changes have affected the attractiveness of heartland shops and the vibrancy of the town and neighbourhood centres. Furthermore, the HDB heartland shops in some towns and neighbourhood centres are finding it difficult to remain competitive, variety of products and services by online retailers, and attractiveness of the shopping environment.

As heartland shops play an important role in servicing the community and enabling residents to age in place, the Singapore government has adopted a three-pronged approach to revitalise HDB heartland shops through the ROS scheme. The ROS scheme comprises the following components:

- co-funding for upgrading of common areas;
- co-funding for optional shopfront improvement works;
- co-funding for promotional events;
- rent-free periods for tenants to renovate their shops; and
- start-up fund for the formation of Merchants' Association.

The ROS scheme is initiated by the ministry based on the feedback received from the stakeholders of the town centres and neighbourhood centres. The merchants' associations for the town centres and neighbourhood centres or HDB retail shops can also make requests to the ministry to spearhead the ROS programme for their centres. Once the ROS is approved by the ministry, the HDB and town council will work closely to coordinate the upgrading works with the merchants' association, shops and community. A working committee comprising representatives from the merchants' association, shops, town council, HDB and grassroots organisations can be formed to coordinate the upgrading works. Depending on the design of the town/neighbourhood centre and requirements of various stakeholders, the working committee will identify the users' requirements and improvement work items for the ROS. The scope of work may entail the following:

- upgrading of shopfront walkways and shop outdoor display areas;
- construction of covered linkways, drop-off porches and vertical blinds;
- upgrading of shopping plaza and multi-purpose hardcourts;
- town/neighbourhood identity landmark/gateway and directional signages;
- lighting and CCTV to town/neighbourhood centres;
- landscaping and gardens; and
- provision of barrier access amenities.

In the ROS scheme, HDB will also reorganise the shops and tenant mix to ensure that the town/neighbourhood centre can better serve the residents. At the same time, there may be a change of tenants or shop ownership or trades in the ROS process. In addition, the government provides a slew of measures to support small and medium-sized enterprises (SMEs), such as direct allocation and rental discount of shops/offices for social enterprises, e-payment solution for coffeeshops, rent-free period for renovation works, rental rebates during upgrading works, and lower electrical upgrading cost. The cost of upgrading for ROS is co-shared between the government and the shop owners.

(e) Other Upgrading Programmes

Besides the NRP, LUP, HIP and ROS, the government has also implemented various *ad-hoc* upgrading programmes, such as private estate upgrading works, electrical load upgrading works for HDB blocks and precincts, and multi-storey carpark upgrading works, including the installation of lifts. These upgrading works are fully funded by the government and do not require the 75% mandate from residents. Thus, the comprehensive suite of town upgrading programmes have rejuvenated many towns. It has also improved the living environment of the residents and increased the vibrancy and inclusiveness of the towns in Singapore.

Chapter 8

Business Continuity Management System and Future Challenges

8.1 Introduction

The town council provides a range of services to ensure that routine maintenance works, cyclical maintenance works, and upgrading works are properly carried out to benefit the residents. While the town council has set up organisational structures to pursue its vision and mission, it is necessary to build resilience in its operations to cope with business continuity disruptions. An example of such disruptions would be the COVID-19 disease outbreak, which has impeded the town council's delivery of services but also represented an opportunity for the town council to build resilience in its operations.

Different crises will have different impacts on town council operations and varying consequences. Thus, it is vital for the town council to develop its own Business Continuity Plan (BCP) to respond to and manage such threats. The adoption of a business continuity management framework such as ISO 22301 (ISO 22301:2019 — Security and Resilience — Business Continuity Management Systems) has facilitated the setting up of a Business Continuity Management System (BCMS) to protect against, reduce the likelihood of occurrence of, prepare for, respond to and recover from disruptions when they arise in the town council. The BCMS will enable the town council to identify potential threats and ascertain its impact on town council operations. The need to effectively respond to threats and safeguard the interests of its stakeholders will also help to build organisational resilience and develop the town council's operational capabilities.

8.2 Business Continuity Management System (BCMS)

As defined by ISO 22301, Business Continuity Management "is a holistic management process that identifies potential threats to an organization and the impacts to business operations those threats, if realized, might cause, and which provides a framework for building organizational resilience with the capability of an effective response that safeguards the interests of its key stakeholders, reputation, brand and value-creating activities".

The 15 People's Action Party (PAP) town councils have adopted a common approach (i.e. ISO 22301: 2019 — Societal Security — Business Continuity Management System — Requirements) to develop their respective BCMSs and plans. Each town council will have to align its vision, mission and business objectives to the BCM framework, so that it can develop a suitable business continuity management framework to reduce the impact of identified threats to its operations and respond with the appropriate operating procedures to facilitate a quick recovery to normal operations. The BCM framework must ensure that the town councils can continue to deliver essential maintenance services during any disruptions that are caused by either man-made or natural disasters, so that it can ensure that the health and safety of residents and stakeholders are not compromised. It will also stipulate the policies, standards and operating procedures that should be implemented to develop and sustain the BCMS.

The key components of a BCMS for a town council comprise the following:

- a BCM Policy;
- people with defined responsibilities for the BCMS;
- management processes (policy, planning, implementation and operation, performance assessment, management review and improvement); and
- documentation providing auditable evidence.

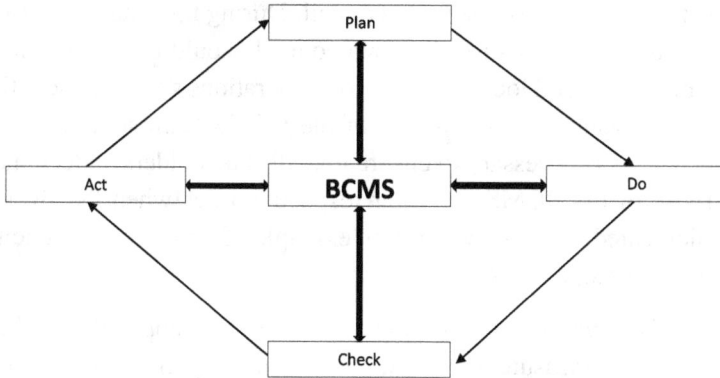

Figure 8.1 Plan–Do–Check–Act Model for BCMS

To align with the requirements of the ISO 22301 standard, the town councils have adopted the "Plan–Do–Check–Act" (PDCA) model to establish and develop their respective BCMSs. The key processes of the PDCA model are set out in Figure 8.1.

- **Plan (establish)**: Establish the business continuity policy, objectives, targets, controls, processes and procedures relevant to improving business continuity, in order to deliver results that align with the organisation's overall policies and objectives.
- **Do (implement and operate)**: Implement and operate the business continuity policy, controls, processes and procedures.
- **Check (monitor and review)**: Monitor and review the actual performances and outcomes against the business continuity policy and objectives, report these results to the management for their review, and ultimately ascertain and authorise the appropriate follow-up action to resolve the challenges faced and improve the BCMS.
- **Act (maintain and improve)**: Maintain and improve the BCMS by taking corrective action based on the results of the management review and reappraising the scope of the BCMS and business continuity policy and objectives.

Using the PCDA model, the BCMS can be developed in seven phases:

1. **Phase 1 — Defining the scope and objectives of the BCMS**: This phase entails the definition of the BCMS with regard to the key

business functions of the town council. During this phase, the BCMS policy and objectives for the town council should be set out, the key business units and location of various operations should be identified, and the organisational structure of the BCMS team should be established. This is necessary to ensure that all stakeholders understand the purpose of the BCMS and their respective roles when the BCMS is implemented. The following is an example of how a town council can define the scope of BCMS:

- **BCMS definition**: The town council shall apply the BCMS to identify, measure, evaluate, control and respond to identified key risks and threats that will prevent the town council from achieving its mission and objectives.
- **BCMS policy**: The town council shall work with its stakeholders to develop a seamless and sustainable town, thus improving the quality of life of its residents and stakeholders. The town council shall also place greater emphasis on the following key areas: such as estate cleanliness, estate maintenance, lift performance, service and conservancy charges collection and arrears management, corporate governance and financial adequacy.
- **BCMS scope**: The BCMS shall apply to both the main and branch offices of the town council and focus on the key town council operations, as shown in Table 8.1.
- **BCMS organisation structure**: The chairperson of the town council can either chair the BCM steering committee or appoint a town councillor to chair the committee. The BCM steering committee shall comprise the chairpersons of the respective standing committees, town councillors and the general manager. The BCM steering committee shall appoint a BCM team comprising the town council general manager, Business Continuity (BC) coordinator, and Business Unit (BU) coordinators. Thereafter, the respective BU coordinators shall appoint their respective disaster response teams, disaster recovery teams and disaster assessment teams, which shall include members from their business units.

2. **Phase 2 — Risk analysis and management**: This phase entails the identification of key risks which will adversely affect the operations and service delivery of the town council. It will highlight the

Table 8.1 Risk Impact on Town Council

Risk Level	Risk Impact	Financial	Business Operations	Legal and Regulatory	Reputation and Image	Social Responsibility and Public Accountability	People	Assets/Information Systems
1	Very low	Financial loss amounting to less than $100,000.	Key processes are unavailable for a very short time period and cause negligible impact on business operations and its ability to fulfil the Minimum Continuity Business objectives (MBCO).	Negligible impact on ability to fulfil contractual and/or statutory obligations.	Negligible or limited adverse impact on reputation and image.	Negligible impact.	No injury or medical treatment required.	Critical assets/systems are unavailable for a very short time period, causing negligible negative impact on organisation's business operations and/or ability to fulfil MBCO.
2	Low	Financial loss amounting between $100,000 and $300,000.	Key processes are unavailable for a very short time period and cause slight impact on business operations and its ability to fulfil the Minimum Continuity Business objectives (MBCO).	Minor impact on ability to fulfil contractual and/or statutory obligations.	Minor negative impact on reputation and image. Some adverse impacts limited to the organisation's stakeholders.	Minor impact.	Minor injury with short-term lost time injury.	Critical assets/systems are unavailable for a short time period, causing negligible negative impact on organisation's business operations and/or ability to fulfil MBCO.

(Continued)

Table 8.1   *(Continued)*

Risk Level	Risk Impact	Financial	Business Operations	Legal and Regulatory	Town Council Impact			
					Reputation and Image	Social Responsibility and Public Accountability	People	Assets/Information Systems
3	Medium	Financial loss amounting between $300,000 and $700,000.	Key processes are unavailable for a moderate time period and cause moderate impact on business operations and its ability to fulfil the Minimum Continuity Business objectives (MBCO).	Warnings, fines and/or regulatory investigations by external agencies.	Moderate negative impact on reputation and image. Negative impact on stakeholder's confidence and/or negative publicity on various forums.	Significant impact.	Injuries, possibly hospitalisation with short-term lost time injury.	Critical assets/systems are unavailable for a moderate time period, causing partial negative impact on organisation's business operations and/or ability to fulfil MBCO.
4	High	Financial loss amounting between $700,000 and $1,000,000.	Key processes are unavailable for a long time period and cause significant negative impact on business operations and its ability to fulfil the Minimum Continuity Business objectives (MBCO).	Lawsuit for damages or termination of contract.	Significant negative publicity and damage to reputation and image. Possible adverse media coverage.	Major impact.	Long-term illness, multiple serious injuries and hospitalisation with long-term lost time injury.	Critical assets/systems are unavailable for a long time period, causing significant negative impact on organisation's business operations and/or ability to fulfil MBCO.

5	Very High	Financial loss amounting to more than $1,000,000.	Key processes are unavailable for an extended time period and cause severe and irreversible negative impact on business operations and total failure to fulfil the Minimum Continuity Business objectives (MBCO).	Multiple lawsuits for damages or termination of contract and may result in termination of operations.	Catastrophic negative publicity and damage to reputation and image. Adverse media coverage both locally and internationally.	Unacceptable impact.	Fatalities or permanent disability.	Critical assets/systems are unavailable for an extended time period, causing severe and irreversible negative impact on organisation's business operations and/or total failure to fulfil MBCO.

likelihood of occurrence of the identified risks and assess their impact on the various operations of the town council. Over the years, the town councils have experienced different types of disruptions and crises. These pose threats to its delivery of services and operations. At the same time, the disruptions to business continuity have resulted in damage to property, sickness and injuries to workers and residents, and financial losses. To formulate a business continuity plan, the council needs to identify the key risks, estimate their potential impact on the town council, and develop a response and recovery framework to restore disrupted services to normalcy. The key steps involved in identifying the risks faced by town councils are listed as follows:

(a) **Step 1**: Identify the key business units of the town council (i.e. finance, estate management and public relations).
(b) **Step 2**: Identify the risks or threats to the key business units.
(c) **Step 3**: Determine and rank the identified risks according to the likelihood of the risk occurring and its potential impact on the business units.
(d) **Step 4**: Decide which risks are acceptable to the town council.
(e) **Step 5**: Adopt appropriate risk treatment measures to manage the risks.
(f) **Step 6**: Estimate the period of disruption caused by each risk and the effectiveness of response and recovery measures in facilitating the resumption of operations.

Based on the experiences of the town councils, the key risks that have an adverse impact on town council operations are as follows:

- **Pandemic/disease outbreaks**: Pandemic or disease outbreaks such as COVID-19 or dengue fever will have an adverse impact on town council operations, affecting its staff, workers, residents and the general public. In these situations, the town councils will have to work closely with the relevant authorities, such as the Ministry of Health or National Environment Agency, to set up measures to prevent the spread of the disease and protocols to manage the affected people. As directed or advised by the ministries or government agencies, the town councils may also have to step up operations to disinfect affected areas during disease outbreaks. In the event of a dengue outbreak, the town councils will conduct extensive inspection and clearing operations to remove breeding sites for mosquitoes in the affected blocks and areas.

- **Cyberattack/IT failures**: Town councils manage the confidential information of their respective residents, shop/hawker stall operators and social communal organisations within the town. Personal and financial data are stored in the computerised finance and estate management systems. Thus, the town council must set up firewalls and IT security protocols to protect the personal data of its clients in accordance with the requirements of the Personal Data Protection Act (PDPA). In today's digital world, data security breaches can cause substantial damage to an organisation. Thus, it is crucial to set up robust firewalls and properly train staff to protect the personal information of residents and stakeholders.
- **Extreme weather conditions (floods, storms and droughts)**: In recent years, the town councils have experienced some extreme weather conditions, such as heavy downpour, strong winds and dry weather. These have caused numerous disruptions to town council operations and towns, and may include instances of flooding, fallen trees and branches, objects falling from heights, water seepages through roofs and façades, and droughts affecting trees and plants. To address these, the town councils will need to take measures to reduce flooding at common areas (by increasing drainage capacity and clearing debris from drain outlets regularly), check the health of trees and prune trees as and when necessary, and choose suitable trees and plants which are more drought-tolerant.
- **Fire**: Every year, an estimated 1,000 incidents of fire occur in residential buildings in Singapore. The causes of fires can be attributed to unattended cooking, indiscriminate disposal of lighted materials, such as cigarette butts and burning charcoal, faulty electrical wirings and appliances, overcharging of electrical appliances or devices (personal mobility device) and arson. These fires can result in the loss of lives and extensive damage to flats and their surroundings.
- **Power outage**: Power disruptions or outages will affect the operations of the town councils, including the lighting, lifts, water pumps and smart facilities management systems. In most cases, such disruptions are minor and may only affect certain blocks. However, in more

serious cases, the effects of these disruptions could be extensive and severely affect the entire town. Key concerns during power outages include the possibility of individuals being trapped in inoperative lifts, patients that require electrical powered devices for medical support, and the general safety of residents. The town councils must ensure that regular testing of its Emergency Battery Operated Power Supply (EBOPS) and Automatic Rescue Device (ARD) for lifts are carried out to ensure that they are functional. and operationally ready. During a power outage, the EBOPS and ARD are important sources of power that can be used to supply power to the lifts and rescue individuals that are trapped therein.

- **Haze**: During the southwest monsoon seasons (between June and October), smoke haze from forest fires in the surrounding regions can be naturally blown towards Singapore and affect the air quality and health of individuals in Singapore. This will affect the air quality and health of people in Singapore. In such situations, the National Environment Agency monitors the air quality through the 24-hour Pollutant Standards Index (PSI) readings daily. The PSI readings are categorised into five ranges: (i) good (0–50), (ii) moderate (51–100), (iii) unhealthy (101–200), (iv) very unhealthy (201–300) and (v) hazardous (above 300). Based on the PSI readings, the National Environment Agency and relevant government agencies will then advise the town councils and general public to take the appropriate measures accordingly.

- **Theft or break-in**: Theft or break-in into town council offices or other secured facilities such as roof tops, water tanks, electrical switch rooms, or pump rooms can cause different degrees of disruptions to town council services. For example, break-ins into the town council office may result in the loss of cash, equipment or documents which could contain personal and confidential information. Theft of town council assets or installations such as fire extinguishers, precast concrete drain cover slabs or metal grilles, and lighting or electric circuit breakers may cause injuries, damage to property and financial loss to the town council.

- **Loss of key appointment holders/vendors**: The loss of key appointment holders such as chairpersons, secretaries, or general managers will affect the operations of the town council, including the progress of ongoing projects. Similarly, the loss of key vendors may also disrupt town council operations, especially for specialist service providers, such as lift firms or IT service providers.

These key risks may have potential adverse impacts on the town council in the following areas, as shown in Table 8.1:

- financial (monetary loss);
- business operations (processes and service delivery);
- legal and regulatory compliance (Town Councils Act and relevant regulations);
- reputation and image of town council/MPs (political impact and goodwill);
- social responsibility and public accountability (corporate governance);
- town councillors, staff, contractors and stakeholders (reputation and well-being);
- town council's assets (fixed and current assets); and
- computerised information systems (hardware and software).

Once the key risks and the relevant impact have been identified, the risk likelihood (Table 8.2) and risk impact of each threat can be determined as shown in Table 8.3. Based on the risk likelihood and risk impact

Table 8.2 Risk Likelihood

Risk Level	Risk Likelihood	Description
1	Very low	Highly unlikely but it may occur in exceptional circumstances. May occur once in 10 years.
2	Low	Not expected, but there is a slight possibility that it may occur at some time. May occur once in 5 years.
3	Medium	May occur at some time as there is a history of casual occurrence. May occur once in 2 years.
4	High	Strong possibility of occurrence as there is a history of frequent occurrence. May occur once a year.
5	Very high	Very likely to occur as there is a history of regular occurrence. May occur once in 3 months.

Table 8.3   Risk Rating Scores of Key Threats/Risks to Town Council

Risk Likelihood	Risk Impact				
	Very Low (1)	Low (2)	Medium (3)	High (4)	Very High (5)
Very low (1)	Theft or break-in (1 × 1 = 1 point)				Extreme weather conditions (1 × 5 = 5 points)
Low (2)			Cyberattack/ IT failures (2 × 3 = 6 points) Power outage (2 × 3 = 6 points)		
Medium (3)			Haze (3 × 3 = 9 points)	Fire (3 × 4 = 12 points)	
High (4)				Disease outbreak/ pandemic (4 × 4 = 16 points)	
Very high (5)					

scores, the overall risk rating scores of the key risks facing town council operations can then be computed and ranked as follows:

(1) Infectious disease/pandemic $= 4 \times 4 = 16$ points (high risk score)
(2) Fire $= 3 \times 4 = 12$ points
(3) Haze $= 3 \times 3 = 9$ points
(4) Power outage $= 2 \times 3 = 6$ points
(5) Cyberattack/IT failures $= 2 \times 3 = 6$ points
(6) Extreme weather conditions $= 1 \times 5 = 5$ points
(7) Theft or break-in $= 1 \times 1 = 1$ point (low risk score)

3. **Phase 3 — Business impact analysis**: This phase entails the identification of business functions that are critical to the continued

Table 8.4 Recovery Time Objectives for Critical Town Council Operations

S/No	Town Council Operations	Time
1	Lift rescue services	8 hours
2	Cleaning and refuse collection	8 hours
3	Maintenance of mechanical and electrical services	8 hours
4	Booking of facilities	8 hours
5	Call centre services	24 hours
6	Public relations	24 hours
7	Lift maintenance	2 days
8	Work order issuance	2 days
9	Managing common areas	2 days
10	Payroll	7 days
11	Service & Conservancy Charges collection	7 days
12	Town improvement projects	21 days
13	Payment to contractors	21 days
14	Procurement	21 days
15	Contract management	21 days
16	Vendor management	21 days
17	Horticulture and landscaping services	21 days

operations of the town council. It also sets out the objectives and priorities for the recovery of these critical business functions. Based on the experiences of the town councils, 11 critical business functions were identified and the Recovery Time Objectives (RTOs) were set as shown in Table 8.4. The RTO refers to the "maximum acceptable length of time that can lapse before the lack of a business function severely impacts the town council".

The recovery of different types of town council services will vary according to the impact of the risks on town council operations and the needs of their residents and stakeholders. Thus, the town councils will have to allocate resources and set up their risk response plans accordingly. These will involve prioritising the types of services to be restored and setting RTOs. As mentioned, based on the collective experiences of the town councils, the recommended RTOs for critical town council operations are listed in Table 8.4.

4. **Phase 4 — Business continuity strategy**: This phase entails the identification of appropriate business recovery strategies for critical business functions and the determination of the resources required to implement the strategies. The details of the recovery strategies are shown in Table 8.5.

5. **Phase 5 — Business continuity plan development**: This phase entails the development of Business Continuity Plans (BCPs) for various scenarios and under different assumptions. It sets out the procedures to be undertaken by the town council upon activation of the BCP plan, as shown in the flowchart in Figure 8.2. The activation is based on the worst-case scenario, which assumes that the main office of the town council is no longer operational due to the adverse effects brought about by the disaster. As such, an alternative site will be set up, so that the town council may continue performing its critical functions and coordinate the business recovery operations. The roles and responsibilities of the Business Continuity Coordinator (BCC), business unit head, recovery team leader and recovery team members will be expressly set out so that everyone will act according to the BCP plan and understand their role when a disaster occurs. The business recovery teams for the respective business units will also be activated to execute the recovery operations until normal operations can be resumed. The business unit recovery procedures are shown in Tables 8.6–8.14.

6. **Phase 6 — Testing and exercising**: This phase entails the documentation of instructions to conduct exercises and test the business continuity plans. Such tests and exercises shall be conducted annually. It shall include tabletop exercises, simulation exercises and call tree notifications. The BCM team will provide a report of the test results and propose recommendations to the BCM steering committee to review its BCMS.

7. **Phase 7 — BCMS review**: This phase entails the review of the BCMS at specified intervals to determine its continued stability, adequacy and effectiveness in satisfying the BCMS requirements. Preventive and corrective action shall be taken to maintain and

Table 8.5 Recovery Strategies for Critical Town Council Functions

S/No	Critical Town Council Functions	Recovery Strategies
1	Lift rescue services	Resume work processes — activate Essential Maintenance Services Unit (EMSU) to take over calls and deploy contractors for urgent cases.
2	Facilities and functions booking	Provide degraded services — activate EMSU to handle enquiries until the setting up of an alternate site for the town council.
3	Cleaning & refuse collection services	Provide degraded services — activate EMSU to take over calls and deploy contractors for urgent cases.
4	Maintenance of mechanical & electrical services	Transfer function/outsource — activate EMSU to take over urgent cases. Town council will take over once its alternate site and call centre is ready.
5	Public relations	Provide degraded services — public relations team will work from home.
6	Call centre services	Provide degraded services — activate EMSU to take over calls and revert to town council once the alternate site and call centre is ready.
7	Lift maintenance	Resume work processes — activate the EMSU to take over calls and deploy contractors for urgent cases.
8	Work order issuance	Resume work processes — property officers will commence function once the alternate site is ready.
9	Managing common areas	Resume work processes — property officers will commence function once the alternate site is ready.
10	Payroll to direct staff	Apply manual process — check and confirm list of personnel employed and make payment by cheque.
11	Service & Conservancy Charges collection	Apply manual process — town council to commence operations once alternate site is ready.

Pre-crisis preparation

- Update and test BCP plans
- Maintain alternate site/command centre/IT disaster recovery site
- Back up critical files and store vital records offsite
- Conduct regular BCP training and awareness

↓

Crisis occurs

↓

Immediate response

- Evacuate, notify and escalate by T + 0.5 hour
- Activate crisis management team by T + 0.5 hours
- Obtain damage assessment result by T + 1 hour
- Declare disaster and activate BCP plan/alternate site/command centre/IT disaster recovery site by T + 1.5 hours

↓

Recovery

- Notify recovery team of crisis management team decisions
- Occupy alternate site/command centre/IT disaster recovery site
- Deliver additional resources to alternate site
- Recover critical business functions

↓

Resumption

- Resume critical business functions
- Continue operations at alternate site
- Salvage and restore critical items at primary site

↓

Restoration

- Re-input backlogged and lost data
- Implement data synchronisation procedures
- Restart normal mode of operation

↓

Restoration

- Return to restored primary location or new premises

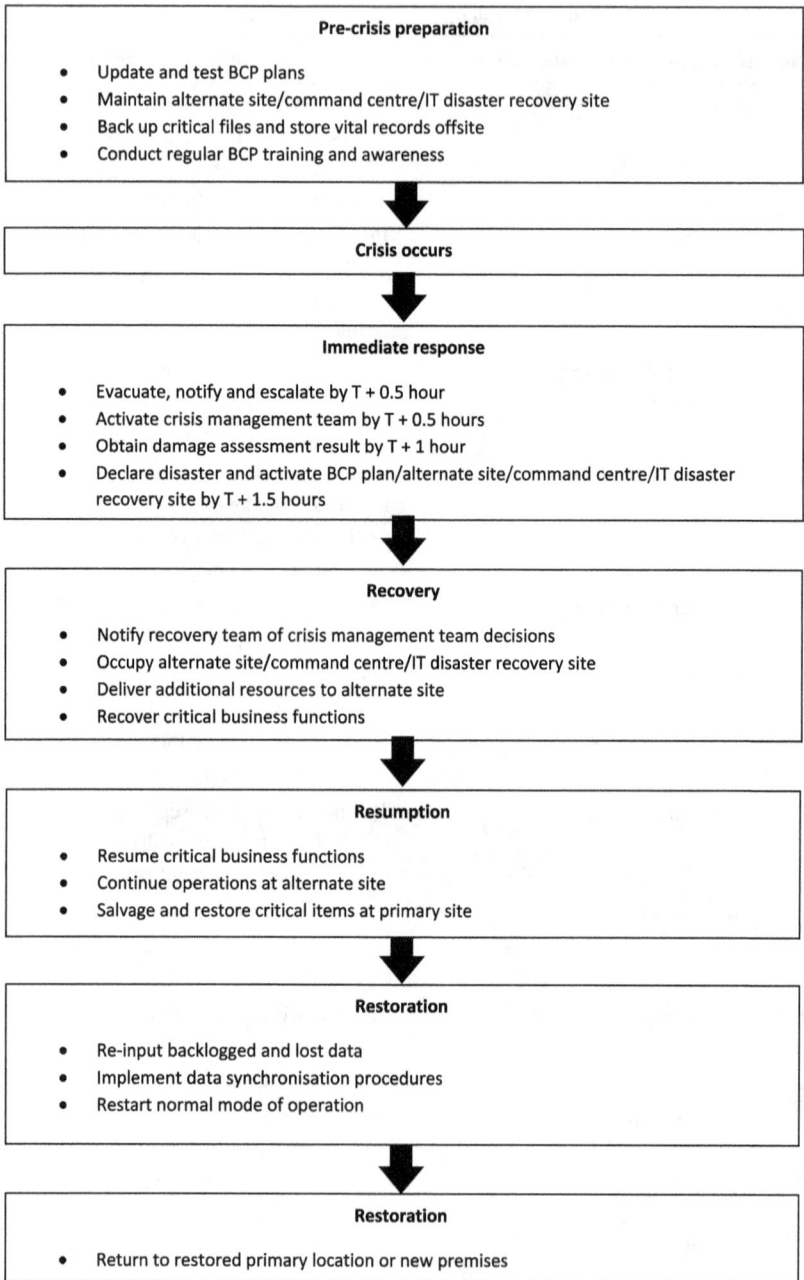

Figure 8.2 Flowchart of Business Continuity Plan Activation

Table 8.6   Business Continuity Plan
(Lift rescue services/lift maintenance)

Action	Estate Management Business Unit	Persons Responsible
What functions to be recovered?	**Lift rescue services/lift maintenance**	• Call centre team • Essential Maintenance Service Unit (EMSU) • Lift Maintenance Unit (LMU) • Property manager • Property officer
Pre-crisis preparation		
How to prepare before crisis?	• Ensure that lift maintenance services are carried out regularly. • Monitor data which may highlight a potential issue with the lift. • Ensure lift maintenance contract specifies the rescue response.	• LMU
Immediate response		
How to respond to a crisis?	• Informed of breakdown by residents or TMS activation. • Activate lift rescue team by call centre/EMSU. • EMSU to highlight urgency to the lift rescue team. • Escalate incident to property manager in charge of block. • Carry out rescue operations.	• Call centre team • Lift rescue team • Property manager/property officer
Recovery and resumption		
Within T + 1 hour		
How to recover operations?	• Make arrangements for residents who may need urgent access to and from their units (medical emergencies). • Place notices by "lift indicator" or notice to advise residents of breakdown/maintenance service. • Lift rescue team to report status to EMSU. • Check and turn on lift by lift company.	• Property officer • Lift company

(*Continued*)

Table 8.6   *(Continued)*

Action	Estate Management Business Unit	Persons Responsible
	Within T + 2 hours	
How to handover operations?	• Submit report from lift company to LMU. • Investigate and submit findings by lift company. • Recommend corrective and preventive action measures to LMU. • LMU to check lift safety before turning on operation. • Remove breakdown notices.	• Lift company • LMU
	Restoration and return	
How to resume normal operations?	• Update EMSU when all services are back to normal. • Prepare the lift breakdown report to EMSU/LMU.	• EMSU • LMU • Lift company

Table 8.7   Business Continuity Plan
(Cleaning and refuse collection services)

Action	Estate Management Business Unit	Persons Responsible
What functions to be recovered?	**Cleaning and refuse collection services**	• Property manager • Property officer • Call centre
	Pre-crisis preparation	
How to prepare before crisis?	• Manage cleaning and refuse collection contracts to attain Service Level Agreement requirements. • Monitor feedback from residents and stakeholders on cleanliness and manage contractors accordingly. • Display notices (including digital display) to inform residents of cleaning and refuse collection services and disruptions, if any.	• Property manager • Property officer

Table 8.7 (*Continued*)

Action	Estate Management Business Unit	Persons Responsible
	Immediate response	
How to respond to a crisis?	• Deploy cleaners and refuse collectors from another division/ward to the affected areas.	• Property manager • Property officer
	Recovery and resumption	
How to recover operations?	• Update the call centre on the situation and status of the cleaning and refuse collection. • Property officers to survey affected areas to identify any potential problems.	• Property manager • Property officer
	Within T + 4 hours	
How to recover operations?	• Inform public relations team to send out a notification to residents on disruption of services through notices or digital display. • Property officer to survey affected areas to identify any potential problems.	• Property manager • Property officer
	Within T + 1 day	
How to recover operations?	Request update from alternate cleaning contractor.	• Property manager • Property officer
	Restoration and return	
How to resume normal operations?	• Inform public relations team to remove all notices on disruption of services. • Update general manager once normal operations resume. • Terminate the temporary (alternate) cleaning contractor services if the existing contractor returns. Otherwise, proceed to appoint a new contractor for the affected areas.	• GM/property manager • Property officer

Table 8.8 Business Continuity Plan
(Maintenance of mechanical and electrical services)

Action	Estate Management Business Unit	Persons Responsible
What functions to be recovered?	**Maintenance of mechanical and electrical services**	• Property manager • Property officer

(*Continued*)

Table 8.8   (*Continued*)

Action	Estate Management Business Unit	Persons Responsible
Pre-crisis preparation		
How to prepare before crisis?	• Manage mechanical and electrical contracts to attain Service Level Agreement requirements. • Monitor feedback from residents and stakeholders on mechanical and electrical services and manage contractors accordingly. • Inform public relations team to prepare notices on disruption of mechanical and electrical services (standard template).	• Property manager • Property officer
Immediate response		
How to respond to a crisis?	• Notify the mechanical and electrical contractor through the call centre (during office hours) and EMSU (after office hours).	• Property manager • Property officer • M & E contractor • EMSU • Call centre
Recovery and resumption		
How to recover operations?	• Contact PowerGrid to check on the status of incoming supply of power. • Contact PUB to check on the status of direct water supply. • Property officer to standby on site.	• Property manager • Property officer
Within T + 4 hours		
How to recover operations?	• Monitor and resolve work urgently. • Turn off power generator for essential services like lift services. • Arrange water wagon to distribute water to residents.	• Property manager • Property officer
Restoration and return		
How to resume normal operations?	• Receive report from PUB/PowerGrid. • Submit report to general manager.	• Property manager • Property officer

Table 8.9 Business Continuity Plan
(Work order issuance)

Action	Estate Management Business Unit	Persons Responsible
What functions to be recovered?	**Work order issuance**	• Property manager • Property officer
	Pre-crisis preparation	
How to prepare before crisis?	• Send out regular reminders on the timeline for issuance of work orders.	• Property manager • Property officer
	Immediate response	
How to respond to a crisis?	• Stop issuance of work order till alternate site is set up.	• Property manager • Property officer
	Recovery and resumption	
	Within T + 1 day	
How to recover operations?	• Relocate and commence operations on alternate site. • Review and ensure that the necessary work orders are issued for work carried out during the crisis.	• Property manager • Property officer
	Restoration and return	
How to resume normal operations?	• Confirm the necessary work orders are issued for work carried out during the crisis period. • Report to general manager.	• Property manager • Property officer

Table 8.10 Business Continuity Plan
(Facilities and function booking)

Action	Estate Management Business Unit	Persons Responsible
What functions to be recovered?	**Facilities and function booking**	• Finance and administration manager
	Pre-crisis preparation	
How to prepare before crisis?	• Set out procedures for manual booking of facilities. • Prepare template for notices advising on crisis situation. • Conduct dry run for crisis situation. • Ensure contract with EMSU has the relevant Service Level Agreement for the switch over.	• Finance and administration manager • Public relations manager • BCP coordinator

(*Continued*)

Table 8.10　(*Continued*)

Action	Estate Management Business Unit	Persons Responsible
	Immediate response	
How to respond to a crisis?	• Inform public relations team to put up notices informing residents of disruption in services. • Transfer all calls to EMSU if possible. If not, call centre to activate EMSU. • Activate finance team to proceed to alternate site.	• Finance and administration manager • Public relations manager • Customer relations assistant
	Recovery and resumption	
	Within T + 4 days	
How to recover operations?	• Call centre team to resume operations at alternate site.	• Property manager • Property officer
	Restoration and return	
How to resume normal operations?	• Update call centre when all services are back to normal. • Inform public relations team and property management team to remove notices for service disruption. • Call centre to resume normal operations at main office. • Provide emotional and physical support if needed.	• Finance and administration manager • Public relations manager • Property manager • Property officer

Table 8.11　Business Continuity Plan (Payroll)

Action	Estate Management Business Unit	Persons Responsible
What functions to be recovered?	**Payroll**	• Finance and administration manager
	Pre-crisis preparation	
How to prepare before crisis?	• Keep an updated register of employees. • Update information regularly.	• Finance and administration manager

Table 8.11 (*Continued*)

Action	Estate Management Business Unit	Persons Responsible
	Recovery and resumption	
	Within T + 3 days	
How to recover operations?	• Confirm accuracy based on the current employee listing. • Inform finance and administration manager to invoke manual procedures if necessary. • Issue cheques if necessary. • Check if cheque signatories are available to sign the cheques. • Keep an inventory of all manual payroll transactions.	• Finance and administration manager • Finance and administration assistant
	Restoration and return	
How to resume normal operations?	• Update manual transactions into the computer system. • Confirm accuracy of database.	• Finance and administration manager • Finance and administration assistant

Table 8.12 Business Continuity Plan
(Service and Conservancy Charges collection)

Action	Estate Management Business Unit	Persons Responsible
What functions to be recovered?	**Service and Conservancy Charges collection (S&CC)**	• Finance and administration team
	Pre-crisis preparation	
How to prepare before crisis?	• Set out procedures for manual collection of S&CC. • Prepare template for notices to advise residents of crisis situation. • Conduct dry run for crisis situation.	• Finance and administration manager • Public relations manager • BCP coordinator

(*Continued*)

Table 8.12   (*Continued*)

Action	Estate Management Business Unit	Persons Responsible
	Immediate response	
How to respond to a crisis?	• Inform finance/call centre team of crisis and the need to implement manual collection. • Instruct finance team to report to alternate site. • Public relations team to put up notices informing residents of disruption in services. • Deploy staff to divert residents who may turn up at the main office to make S&CC payment.	• Finance and administration manager • Public relations manager • Customer Relations Assistant • Property manager • Property officer
	Recovery and resumption	
	Within T + 1 hour	
How to recover operations?	• Assess the situation at main office to see if further crowd control measures are needed. • Inform public relations team to update situation on the town council website.	• Finance and administration manager • Public relations manager
	Restoration and return	
How to resume normal operations?	• Inform public relations team to update residents via website or notices once operations are back to normal. • Advise all staff to return back to main office.	• Finance and administration manager

Table 8.13   Business Continuity Plan
(Public relations)

Action	Public Relations Business Unit	Persons Responsible
What functions to be recovered?	**Public relations**	• Public relations manager • Public relations executive
	Pre-crisis preparation	
How to prepare before crisis?	• Prepare template of press statements for response to crisis.	• General manager • Public relations manager

Table 8.13   (*Continued*)

Action	Public Relations Business Unit	Persons Responsible
	Immediate response	
How to respond to a crisis?	• Assess damage and accuracy of crisis. • Ensure "keywords" for the crisis are up to date via social media listening tools. • Advise general manager to escalate to town council chairman, if necessary. • Draft media response to crisis. • Prepare notices to inform residents of crisis via digital display panel or website.	• Public relations manager • Public relations executive
	Recovery and resumption	
	Within T + 1 hour to T + 8 hours	
How to recover operations?	• Release press statement (if restoration takes considerable time). • Update on town council website.	• Finance and administration manager • Public relations manager
	Restoration and return	
How to resume normal operations?	• Inform public relations team to update residents via website or notices once operations are back to normal. • Advise all staff to return back to main office.	• Finance and administration manager

Table 8.14   Business Continuity Plan
(Call centre)

Action	Estate Management Business Unit	Persons Responsible
What functions to be recovered?	**Call centre**	• Public relations manager • Call centre team
	Pre-crisis preparation	
How to prepare before crisis?	• Establish contractual arrangement for switch-over with vendor. • Identify procurement and timeline for IP phones from vendor.	• General manager • Public relations manager

(*Continued*)

Table 8.14 *(Continued)*

Action	Estate Management Business Unit	Persons Responsible
Immediate response		
How to respond to a crisis?	• Inform phone system vendor to route to EMSU. • Inform EMSU of the routing to them. • Activate the setup of alternate site for call centre team. • Access email and feedback system at alternate site.	• Public relations manager • Public relations executive
Recovery and resumption		
Within T + 1 day		
How to recover operations?	• Route incoming calls back to main office. • Resumption of access to feedback and email systems by call centre team at main office.	• Finance and administration manager • Public relations manager
Restoration and return		
How to resume normal operations?	• Ensure all computers and phone connections are up. • Provide emotional and physical support if necessary.	• Finance and administration manager

improve the effectiveness and efficiency of the BCMS. The BCMS review shall determine the following:

(a) what needs to be monitored and measured;
(b) the methods for monitoring, measuring, analysing, and evaluating (as the case may be) to ensure valid results;
(c) when the monitoring and measuring shall be performed; and
(d) when the results from monitoring and measurement shall be analysed and evaluated.

8.3 Benefits of Business Continuity Management System

The development of BCMS for town councils will increase its resilience, reduce adverse impacts and enable town councils to continue their operations and deliver essential services to fulfil the needs of its residents and stakeholders. The key benefits of the BCMS are as follows:

- **Increase resilience**: It helps to increase the resilience of the town councils against any disruptions, thus enabling town councils to continue the delivery of their essential services during disruptions. The BCMS also equips the town councils to better respond to crises and facilitates the recovery of critical town council functions to normal operations.
- **Build confidence**: It builds confidence and trust among the stakeholders and staff of the town councils. This enables the council members and staff to better respond to the threats and win the trust of residents and stakeholders. The morale and confidence of the council members and staff will also be raised with the implementation of the BCMS.
- **Continuity of services**: It ensures that essential services of the town councils are not adversely affected. Appropriate resources can be set aside to ensure the continuity of essential services, thus ameliorating the inconvenience caused to residents and stakeholders.
- **Corporate governance**: It sets out good corporate governance protocol and practices so that town councils can allocate resources to manage disruptions. This will provide more transparency and public accountability. The BCMS provides a framework to ensure that resources are efficiently and effectively utilised when a crisis occurs, and actions are taken to ensure that operations resume as per normal.
- **Branding and image**: The effective implementation of the BCMS during disruptions will enhance the branding of the town councils and reinforce the image that the town councils remain resilient and reliable despite any disruptions it might face. The town councils will also gain more trust and confidence from their stakeholders.

8.4 Future Challenges

(a) Politics and talent retention

Since its formation in 1988, the town councils have undergone a transformation journey to become more "political in nature". At the outset, town councils were primarily tasked with performing the decentralised function of maintaining the HDB estates on behalf of the HDB. However, over the years, elected MPs who manage town councils have realised that the town councils play a key role in implementing improvement projects to enhance the living environment of residents. In addition, if the town councils are able to address the needs and aspirations of residents, these residents will likely be appreciative of such efforts, which in turn helps the elected MPs gain political mileage.

Although many town councils have successfully engaged residents and implemented meaningful improvement projects, some town councils have found it challenging to satisfy the needs and aspirations of its residents, either due to corporate governance lapses or a failure to deliver the services it has promised residents. The annual Town Council Management Report (TCMR) serves as a good indicator of the success of the town council, and MPs are often anxious to find out how their respective town councils have performed. Needless to say, town councils that have failed to fulfill the key performance indicators of the TCMR are likely to have lost the trust and confidence of some residents. In turn, it is entirely possible that the respective elected MPs will also lose political mileage due to the poor performance of the town council.

As public opinion of an MP is inextricably linked to the performance of his or her town council, MPs may encourage the town council staff to improve on the delivery of its services, but this may instead place undue pressure on the staff and affect the overall morale of the team. As the management of the town council requires both technical knowledge and experience in the field, without a well-trained and experienced pool of town council staff, it may be difficult for town councils to continue effectively and efficiently serving residents in future. Consequently, as mentioned, a failure by a town council to fulfill the needs of residents could potentially impact the public opinion on the relevant MP.

Very few organisations have the abilities to manage one million complaints every year, and the ability of town councils to do so can be attributed to the tireless efforts of its staff. Each and every town council staff plays a pivotal role in managing the demands and expectations of elected MPs, residents and various stakeholders to achieve a win–win–win outcome. The complex nature of the job, coupled with an increasingly competitive job market has thus made it difficult for town councils to retain skillful and experienced property managers and officers and attract new talent to help manage the estates. With rising expectations of residents and stakeholders, it will be a challenge for town councils to retain talent to better serve residents in the future.

(b) **Resilience**

The experience of COVID-19 has highlighted the importance of building resilience in town councils in order to ensure the delivery of essential services during a crisis. The impact of climate change has also posed new challenges to town councils. Extreme weather conditions such as heavy rain, strong winds or extreme heat have also affected residents, workers and the built environment of the town. For instance, flash floods have disrupted town council operations and caused damage to property and inconvenience to residents. As such, town councils will have to work closely with the relevant authorities, such as Public Utilities Board (PUB) and National Environment Agency (NEA), to build water retention and drainage facilities in the estates. In addition to the yearly outbreaks of dengue fever, the town councils have also had to deal with the challenges that are attributable to the spread of highly infectious diseases (i.e. SARS and COVID-19). These outbreaks have spurred town councils to reorganise their operations and develop different business continuity plans to reduce disruptions of service delivery. For example, town councils have organised different teams and set up alternate town council offices to better respond to disease outbreaks. The town councils have also formed their respective business continuity teams to coordinate the activation of their business continuity plans when crisis or disaster occurs.

(c) **Smart facilities management**

The advent of technology and digitalisation in facilities management has only be expedited by the COVID-19 outbreak. Many town councils are implementing and exploring smart facilities management solutions in their respective towns. Potential areas in which smart solutions can be implemented include digital databases for property and facilities, Building Information Modelling (BIM) and digital twins, management information systems (dashboard management systems), e-procurement and submission systems, e-invoicing and payments, digital estate inspection systems, contractor's performance evaluation systems, safety and alert systems, utilities monitoring systems, smart devices and robot deployments. Depending on the future needs of residents, the town councils will have to map out suitable smart township solutions. There are three desired outcomes that the town councils can focus on when implementing smart township solutions. These are (i) digitalisation of work processes to improve efficiency, (ii) optimisation of building systems to save costs, and (iii) integration of smart solutions to provide better quality of services. These smart township solutions should also have measurable outcomes that can be closely monitored for further improvements.

The town councils have already started deploying drones to inspect the façades when conducting repairs and redecoration works. In addition, there are other potential areas where robots can be deployed to enhance safety, security or the delivery of services. For instance, robots that have been built to clean and disinfect surfaces can be deployed at common properties and lift cars, whereas robots built for the purposes of surveillance can be used to check the structural integrity of buildings. The installation of smart CCTV and lift surveillance systems can also enhance the safety and security of estates. Ultimately, the adoption of smart township solutions will help MPs and town councils satisfy the needs of residents in the future.

In conclusion, the secret recipe to successful township management is political commitment, strong partnerships and professional practice. It is also imperative for the town council to continue attracting and retaining talent to sustain its efforts in making every town "a successful, sustainable and liveable town" for all Singaporeans.

Index

Accounting and financial services, 59
Administrative and secretarial
  services, 59
Alert Alarm System (AAS), 75
Animal/pet nuisance, 111
Annual accounts, 38
Annual Work Plan, 3
Audit, 39
Audit Committee, 24, 31, 62
Automatic Rescue Device (ARD), 73

Banner post design, 137
BCM framework, 154
BCM policy, 154
BCMS definition, 156
BCMS organisation structure, 156
BCMS scope, 156
Booster pumps, 74
Branding and image, 179
Budgeting and planning, 51
Budget preparation, 66
Building and Construction Authority
  (BCA), 8
Building maintenance, 3
Build rapport, 16
Build-To-Order (BTO) flats, 139

Business Continuity Management
  System (BCMS), 153
Business Continuity Plans (BCPs),
  17
By-election, 4
By-laws, 36, 78

Carpark lightings, 73
Citizens' Consultative Committee
  (CCC), 7, 131
Clean and green, 10
Clean and serviceable condition, 71
Code of Governance, 48
Codes of Practice, 73
Colour scheme, 137
Common property, 3
Communication, 64
Community Improvement Projects
  Committee (CIPC), 131
Complex problems, 102
Composition of offences, 41
Condition survey, 68
Conservancy and cleaning work, 72
Conservancy and service charges, 39
Continuity of services, 179
Contracts Committee, 31, 24

Corporate communication services, 59
Corporate governance, 5, 10, 18, 179
Crises, 153
Customer satisfaction, 60
Customer service, 19
Customer service contact points, 91
Customer service delivery, 10, 64
Customer service lapses, 90
Customer service qualities, 93
Customer service toolkits, 93
Cyberattack, 17
Cyberattack/IT failures, 160
Cyclical maintenance, 119

Damage to common property, 81
Damage to turf, 81
Data privacy and protection, 50
Delegation of powers, 37
Detain, 81
Directional signage, 136
Direct management, 58
Disease outbreaks, 17
Dumping and renovation debris, 45, 80

Educational institutions, 8
Education campaigns, 64
Electrical installations, 73
Electrical works, 73
Emergency Battery Operated Power Supply (EBOPS), 74
Enforcement actions, 63
Enhancement for Active Seniors (EASE), 141
Environmental, Social and Governance (ESG), 11
Essential Maintenance Services Unit (EMSU), 63, 74
Estate cleanliness, 18

Estate Committee, 31, 24
Estate improvement work, 3
Estate Inspection System (EIS), 81
Estate maintenance, 18
Estate Maintenance Committee, 63
Estate management policies, 79
Estate signs, 74
Estate supplies, 76
Estate Upgrading Committee, 63
Estate Upgrading Programme (EUP), 139, 141
Estate upgrading work, 3
Estimates, 38
Extreme weather conditions, 17, 161

Façade design, 137
Facilities and amenities, 10
Facilities management, 3
Feedback channels, 63
Finance and Administration Management, 42
Finance Committee, 24, 31, 62
Financial health, 10
Financial policies, 62, 79
Financial rules, 39
Fines, 39
Fire, 17, 161
Fire protection, 74

Gazette, 55
Good relations, 64
Government agencies, 8
Grass-cutting, 72
Grassroots leaders, 5
Grassroots organisations, 5
Group Representation Constituencies (GRCs), 1
GST subvention claims, 42

Hawker stallholders, 7, 9
Haze, 162
High-rise littering, 113
Home Improvement Programme
  (HIP), 16, 140
Home ownership, 2
Horticulture, 72
Housing and Development Board
  (HDB) flats, 1, 8
Housing policies and programmes, 2
Human resources, 51
Hybrid approach, 58

Illegal parking, 81
Image, 10, 64
Improvement projects, 4, 16
Income tax returns, 42
Increase resilience, 178
Integrated Estate Management
  System (IEMS), 17, 73
Interim Upgrading Programme (IUP),
  140
Internal audit, 50
Internal controls, 62
Internal controls and processes, 50
Investment, 52
ISO 22301:2019, 153, 154

Key appointment holders/vendors,
  162
Key desired outcomes, 9
Key Performance Indicators, 17
Key stakeholders, 4

Landmark signage, 136
Landscape design, 137
Land Transport Authority (LTA), 8
Licensed Electrical Worker (LEW), 73
Life cycle, 15

Lift dashboard management system,
  19
Lift Enhancement Programme (LEP),
  142
Lift maintenance work, 73
Lift performance, 18, 19
Lift Performance Management
  System, 17
Lift Replacement Fund (LRF), 42
Lift Surveillance System (LSS), 74
Lift Telemonitoring System (LTMS),
  73
Lift Upgrading Programme (LUP),
  16, 140

Maintenance management services,
  58
Maintenance policies, 78
Maintenance standards, 71
Main Upgrading Programme (MUP),
  140
Managing Agent, 58
Master plan, 3, 63
Mechanical fan, 75
Media, 9
Media relations, 64
Members of Parliament (MPs), 1
Mental health issues, 115
Merchants' associations, 7
Municipal, 8
Municipal Services Office (MSO), 8,
  14, 18

National Environment Agency
  (NEA), 8
National Parks Board (NParks), 8
Natural or man-made disasters, 17
Needs and aspirations, 139
Neighbour dispute, 109

Neighbourhood centres, 7
Neighbourhood Renewal Programme
    (NRP), 16, 141
Newsletters, 64
Noise nuisance, 105
Non-government organisations, 8
"No wrong door" policy, 14

Obstruction, 107
Obstruction of common property, 80
One Service Mobile App, 14
Optional services, 60
Ownership, 129

Painting, 74
Pandemic/disease outbreaks, 160
Parliamentary general election, 4
Partnership, 10
Performance management, 52
Personal liability, 40
Pest control, 74
Plumbing, 73
Policies and by-laws, 2
Political, 55
Politics and talent retention, 179
Power outage, 17, 161
Precinct naming, 137
Preparatory works, 58
Price Quality Method (PQM), 16, 126
Price score, 127
Procurement, 16, 52
Procurement policies, 79
Procurement processes, 63
Professional bodies, 8
Professional etiquette, 95
Project Committee, 31, 24
Property tax, 44
Protection from personal liability, 41

Public housing development, 1
Publicity and Public Relations
    Committee, 64
Publicity Committee, 31, 24
Public relations, 117
Public relations work, 3
Public Utilities Board (PUB), 8

Quality score, 127
Quorum, 20

Record keeping, 50
Refuse chute flushing system, 74
Refuse handling equipment, 75
Religious organisations, 8
Resident engagement, 117
Residential and commercial
    property, 4
Residents' Committee (RC), 7
Residents' Network (RN), 7
Resilience, 181
Revitalisation of Shops Scheme
    (ROS), 16, 141
Risk management, 50
Risks, 62
Roller doors, 75
Routine maintenance, 71
Routine maintenance
    management, 15

Safe and secure, 10
Safety inspection, 75
Sanitary, 73
Security and resilience, 153
Selective En Bloc Redevelopment
    Scheme (SERS), 141
Sense of belonging, 2
Service and conservancy charges, 62

Shop owners, 9
Singapore, 1
Singapore Civil Defence Force
  (SCDF), 8
Singapore Police Force (SPF), 8
Singapore's public housing, 1
Singapore Standards, 73
Singapore Standard SS 533: 2007, 72
Single Member Constituencies
  (SMCs), 1, 56
Sinking funds, 15
Smart facilities management, 181
Social media, 9
Social service agencies, 8
SS 550:2009, 73
Standard design, 137
Standard Operating Procedures
  (SOPs), 63
Standing committees, 20, 31
Standing orders, 20, 36
Structure, 55
Submersible pumps, 74
Supplementary budget, 69
Sustainability, 128
Sustainability Report, 18, 19

Temporary Occupation Licence
  (TOL), 3
Tender and Contracts Committee, 63
Terrorist attacks, 17
Theft or break-in, 162
Thematic vision, 137
Total PQM score, 127
Town centres, 7
Town Council Annual Report, 18, 19
Town Council by-laws, 44

Town Council Computer
  Management System (TCMS), 78
Town Council Fund, 37
Town Council governance, 27
Town Councillors, 5
Town Council Management Report
  (TCMR), 1
Town Council Plan, 49, 129
Town Councils Act, 11
Town Council setup, 55
Town Councils Financial Rules,
  11, 42
Town identity, 136
Town Improvement Project, 129, 130
Town upgrading, 139
Trade associations, 8
Transfer and diverter pumps, 74
Transfer of surpluses, 38

Unlawful parking, 47
Upgrading of estate policies, 80
Urban Redevelopment Authority of
  Singapore (URA), 8
Users' requirements, 134

Vendor management, 52
Ventilation system, 75
Vision and mission, 9

Water dispenser, 75
Water seepage, 102
Water tank, 73
Whistleblowing, 51
Work Order System, 88

10-year rolling plan, 119

www.ingramcontent.com/pod-product-compliance
Lightning Source LLC
Chambersburg PA
CBHW061250220326
41599CB00028B/5599